The 42 Laws of Wisdom

The 42 Laws of Wisdom

Keys to Spiritual Alignment

By Ancient The Architect

With the intention of restoring Balance…

The 42 Laws of Wisdom: Keys to Spiritual Alignment
Copyright © 2024 by Ancient the Architect
Cover Design and Cover Art © 2024 by Ancient the Architect
Published by Health Is Luxury LLC
Hartford, CT, USA

All rights reserved. No part of this publication may be reproduced, distributed, or transmitted in any form or by any means, including photocopying, recording, or other electronic or mechanical methods, without the prior written permission of the publisher, except in the case of brief quotations embodied in critical reviews and certain other noncommercial uses permitted by copyright law.

For permission requests, inquiries, and other requests, please contact:
Health Is Luxury LLC
Email: yourhealthisluxury@gmail.com

ISBN: 9798992210217

Disclaimer:
This book is intended for informational and educational purposes only. The author and publisher assume no responsibility for any outcomes resulting from the application of the information presented herein. Readers are encouraged to seek professional advice for individual concerns. The spiritual perspectives in this book are based on historical interpretations and personal insights and are not intended to replace or contradict any religious beliefs or practices.

Table of Contents

Preface

- Introduction to Ma'at's Teachings
- The Influence of Ra, Thoth, and Ma'at

Chapter 1: The Law of Virtue
Chapter 2: The Law of Gratitude
Chapter 3: The Law of Peace
Chapter 4: The Law of Respect
Chapter 5: The Law of the Sacredness of Life
Chapter 6: The Law of Genuine Offerings
Chapter 7: The Law of Truth
Chapter 8: The Law of the Reverence for Altars
Chapter 9: The Law of Sincerity
Chapter 10: The Law of Moderation
Chapter 11: The Law of Good Intentions
Chapter 12: The Law of Peaceful Relations
Chapter 13: The Law of Reverence for Animal Life
Chapter 14: The Law of Trustworthiness
Chapter 15: The Law of Sacred Earthkeeping
Chapter 16: The Law of Inner Wisdom
Chapter 17: The Law of Positive Speech
Chapter 18: The Law of Emotional Balance
Chapter 19: The Law of Trust
Chapter 20: The Law of Purity
Chapter 21: The Law of Joy
Chapter 22: The Law of Effort
Chapter 23: The Law of Compassionate Communication
Chapter 24: The Law of Opposing Opinions

Chapter 25: The Law of Harmony
Chapter 26: The Law of Laughter
Chapter 27: The Law of Openness to Love
Chapter 28: The Law of Forgiveness
Chapter 29: The Law of Kindness
Chapter 30: The Law of Considerate Conduct
Chapter 31: The Law of Acceptance
Chapter 32: The Law of Inner Guidance
Chapter 33: The Law of Conversing with Awareness
Chapter 34: The Law of Goodness
Chapter 35: The Law of Blessings
Chapter 36: The Law of Pure Waters
Chapter 37: The Law of Speaking with Good Intent
Chapter 38: The Law of Divine Duality
Chapter 39: The Law of Humility
Chapter 40: The Law of Integrity
Chapter 41: The Law of Self-Reliance
Chapter 42: The Law of Embracing ***The All***

Conclusion: Walking the Path of Wisdom

- Reflecting on the 42 Laws
- Embracing Divine Wisdom and Unity

Preface: Embracing the Divine Wisdom of Ma'at

This book is a journey into the sacred wisdom of the 42 principles of Ma'at, an alchemical process of aligning with the divine laws that correspond to the ancient 42 Negative Confessions. These principles are the spiritual foundations for those seeking harmony with divine order, personal integrity, and inner growth. By embodying these laws (which we may refer to in this book at times as the "42 Laws of Ma'at"), we cultivate the virtues needed to balance our heart against the feather of truth. Each principle serves as a conscious reflection of the inner work required to dissolve barriers, transform the soul, and prepare for the final judgment, where one's heart is weighed in alignment with Ma'at's eternal truth. Drawing from ancient Egyptian philosophy and complemented by selected biblical verses, each chapter is an exploration of profound truths that have guided humanity for millennia. These teachings reflect the harmonious interplay between Ra, the divine source of life and illumination; Thoth, the embodiment of divine intellect and wisdom; and Ma'at, the essence of truth, balance, and cosmic justice. Together, these deities symbolize the fundamental elements of creation, knowledge, and moral order.

The ***42 Laws of Wisdom*** encourage us to live with integrity, pursue wisdom, and recognize our inherent connection to the cosmos. By embracing these laws, we acknowledge our role as co-creators within the vast expanse of the All—the infinite, unknowable source from which everything emanates. Through these teachings, we come to understand that every thought, action, and word reverberates throughout the universe, influencing the collective harmony.

This book delves into the metaphysical, philosophical, and esoteric dimensions of each law, allowing readers to not only understand the teachings of Ma'at but also to apply them in their lives. Whether in personal, interpersonal, educational, or entrepreneurial pursuits, these laws serve as a foundation for living a successful, purposeful life. As you read through these pages, may you be inspired to embody these principles and walk the path of wisdom, unity, and spiritual fulfillment.

Ra: The Supreme Self and Creative Principle

In Egyptian metaphysics, **Ra** is understood as the embodiment of the Supreme Self or the Higher Self. This principle represents the ultimate creative force that brought all things into being. Ra declares, "I am he who came into being in the form of the Indwelling Self (Khepera)". This suggests a manifestation of the *Logos*, or divine word, indicating that Ra is the initiator of creation, transforming the latent potential of the cosmos into active existence. In this view, Ra serves as both the unmanifest source and the manifest world, bridging the gap between nothingness and creation.

The passage highlights that Ra existed before Heaven, Earth, and all other entities, emerging from a state of inactivity (Nu, or the primordial waters of chaos). This aligns with the Hermetic concept that underlies Egyptian metaphysics: the presence of a Substantial Reality behind all outward appearances. Ra is this unchanging essence that remains constant even as all things in the universe are in flux.

Moreover, the number 363, associated with Ra, signifies the Divine Triad of Will, Wisdom, and Action, reflecting the completion of a cosmic cycle. This number is symbolic of the cycle of manifestation through twelve stages, which encompass the dual aspects of spirit and matter, culminating in creation.

The reference to "the year 363" marks a point in the cycle when the Logos or Sun God enters a state of negation, symbolizing the dualities of light and shadow, good and evil, and attraction and repulsion. This stage represents the determination of a solar system to proceed forth, where Ra, as the Ever-Living, manifests through a process that is constantly balanced by divine order and sacrifice. These manifest in dualities (Spirit-matter) and are part of a cosmic cycle, which reflects both completion and the perpetual cycle of birth, death, and rebirth. This ongoing rhythm emphasizes the principle of duality, where opposites (such as light and darkness) play an essential role in maintaining cosmic balance.

The significance of Ra in this context of the 42 Laws is that Ra embodies **self-reliance and the creative power** fundamental to achieving divine harmony. As the Supreme Self and Higher Will, Ra is a symbol of how personal empowerment and divine inspiration are interwoven. Through these 42 Laws, practitioners strive to embody aspects of Ra's essence—creative, balanced, and in harmony with the divine flow.

This synthesis of Ra as both the indwelling and expansive force provides a profound connection to the 42 Laws. Ra represents the ultimate source from which these laws are derived, highlighting how each law guides one toward embodying aspects of this creative and sustaining force. Now that we have a foundation on Ra, please proceed with the additional pages on Thoth and Ma'at, and we can continue to expand this metaphysical framework in alignment with the principles of the 42 Laws.

Thoth: The Divine Mind, Mediator of Wisdom, and Embodiment of Logos

Hermes, or the Egyptian Thoth, represents the *Divine Mind* and functions as an intermediary between the *higher and lower natures*. He embodies logos, the living Word, and serves as a symbol of *intellectual illumination* and *spiritual wisdom*. As the *heart and tongue of Ra*, Thoth is both the *intellectual capacity* and *expression of divine will*—connecting abstract cosmic principles to the physical realm.

In the metaphysical sense, Thoth's role is twofold: he is the *source of divine thought* and the *conduit for expression*. He embodies *creative intelligence*, acting as the force that translates the potential within Ra into manifest reality. In this way, Thoth symbolizes *mental clarity, intuitive understanding, and intellectual discernment*. His association with logos indicates that he is the principle through which divine ideas are structured, organized, and communicated in the material world. He not only bridges *spiritual concepts* with tangible actions but also ensures that the *moral order* is maintained through the *power of language and wisdom*.

Thoth also represents *the art of knowledge and the sciences*, attributed as the *scribe of the gods* and the inventor of all *arts and sciences*. This aligns with the 42 Laws of Ma'at in that it reflects the *importance of self-mastery and intellectual development*. Thoth's association with the *written word* and *record-keeping* symbolizes the idea that our actions are recorded and that living according to Ma'at is essential for maintaining harmony within the self and the universe.

Thoth's Connection to the 42 Laws of Ma'at

The principles of Ma'at can be seen as laws that Thoth, through his association with *order and knowledge,* upholds. He reinforces the *importance of truth, balance, and wisdom* in human life. Thoth, as the *mindful communicator,* reminds us to engage thoughtfully, to reflect on the truth behind appearances, and to act with conscious awareness. His guidance encourages us to cultivate intellectual and intuitive balance and to recognize the *divine potential* within ourselves.

Through the figure of Thoth, the 42 Laws of Ma'at emphasize:

1. **Intellectual Responsibility** - Thoth shows that mastery of self comes through knowledge, and so the laws guide us to develop our minds and use them in service of divine principles.
2. **Spiritual Communication** - Just as Thoth translates the will of Ra into reality, we are to embody and express the essence of Ma'at in our actions, words, and thoughts. This means speaking with *integrity* and using *knowledge to uplift.*
3. **Harmony through Wisdom** - Thoth's role as a mediator between higher and lower realms underscores the importance of harmonizing our spiritual and physical lives. The 42 Laws of Ma'at offer a framework that encourages *balanced living,* integrating *divine wisdom* into everyday interactions.

In conclusion, Thoth represents the *divine intellect* and *wisdom* necessary to apply Ma'at's laws effectively. He teaches that *self-realization and moral living* are pathways to divine connection, and he embodies the *art of living with higher consciousness.* The laws serve as guideposts, echoing Thoth's example of embodying *truth and wisdom* in every thought and action, grounding our spiritual aspirations in the material world with integrity and purpose.

Ma'at: The Embodiment of Divine Order and Cosmic Law

Ma'at, the daughter of Ra and wife of Thoth, is the divine embodiment of absolute law, justice, and order. Her role is central to the function of the universe and is intrinsically linked to the law of karma. She represents an unchanging cosmic principle that governs both the moral and natural worlds. In Egyptian cosmology, Ma'at is essential to maintaining balance across all realms, guiding the gods, and influencing human affairs.

Ma'at's essence is more than just justice in the human sense; she encompasses the orderly functioning of the cosmos. She is the regulator of moral rectitude, truth, and right action, manifesting the ideals that humanity should strive to embody. This aligns her directly with the concept of karma, the universal law that ensures every action is accounted for and balanced.

The Feather of Ma'at: Symbol of Spiritual Balance and Ephemeral Life

The feather of Ma'at, often depicted as an ostrich feather, is a profound symbol in ancient Egyptian thought. During the weighing of the heart ceremony, the feather was used to measure the soul's purity and alignment with truth. This emphasizes the importance of purity in actions, thoughts, and intentions.

The feather symbolizes the transient, ephemeral nature of physical existence. It signifies that the personality, tied to the lower planes of being, is a temporary aspect of the soul's journey. Just as a feather can be wafted away, the physical self must eventually dissolve, leaving only the soul's alignment with divine order to determine its place in the afterlife. The feather, therefore, is a reminder of the impermanent nature of life and the ultimate importance of living in harmony with cosmic laws.

By embodying the qualities of Ma'at, individuals align themselves with this higher order, allowing their souls to resonate with truth and balance. The feather also serves as a symbol of liberation from the material world, indicating that true liberation comes from adhering to Ma'at's principles and shedding the illusions of the ego.

Together, Ma'at and her feather symbolize the path of spiritual alignment, personal responsibility, and the pursuit of divine harmony. They guide individuals to live with integrity, honor, and respect for the cosmic balance, ensuring that their actions contribute positively to the universe's ongoing process of creation and transformation.

Ra: The Divine Source and the Life-Giver

Ra represents the supreme creative force, the origin of all existence, and the sustainer of the cosmos. As the ultimate source, Ra embodies the foundational energy from which everything emerges. His role is to be the light that brings forth life, establishing the cosmic order that governs the universe. In a metaphysical sense, Ra is the ultimate expression of the divine self, manifesting as the Supreme Self or the Higher Self within each being. He brings forth creation from a state of latency, symbolizing the emergence of life from pure potential.

Thoth: The Divine Mind and Interpreter of Universal Law

Thoth, often regarded as the Egyptian counterpart to Hermes, symbolizes divine intellect, wisdom, and the higher mind. He is the mediator between Ra and Ma'at, bridging the spiritual and material worlds. Thoth embodies the principle of divine wisdom, enabling us to interpret and understand the cosmic order established by Ra. Known as the scribe of the gods, Thoth is responsible for translating the intentions of Ra into

tangible forms, such as knowledge, language, and sacred texts. Through Thoth, the abstract truths of Ra become accessible, allowing us to comprehend and align ourselves with divine will.

Ma'at: The Divine Order and Balance of the Cosmos

Ma'at represents the ultimate expression of justice, balance, and moral rectitude. She is the law by which the universe operates, the divine order that ensures all things are in harmony. Ma'at's essence is reflected in the principles of truth, integrity, and cosmic balance. As the daughter of Ra, she embodies his order and extends it to the moral and spiritual dimensions of human existence. Ma'at ensures that the universe functions in equilibrium, guiding individuals to live in accordance with universal laws. Her role is not only to maintain order but also to act as the spiritual standard by which all beings are measured.

The Interconnectedness of Ra, Thoth, and Ma'at

Ra, Thoth, and Ma'at together form a trinity that upholds and manifests divine order in the universe. They are distinct but interdependent aspects of the divine:

- **Ra and Ma'at**: Ra establishes the fundamental order of the cosmos, and Ma'at maintains it. Ra's light gives life, while Ma'at's principles ensure that life functions within a harmonious structure. In a sense, Ra is the source of creation, and Ma'at is the means by which creation is sustained and kept in balance. Ma'at's role as the keeper of order is a direct extension of Ra's purpose as the origin of all life. Without Ma'at, Ra's creation would fall into chaos, lacking the structure necessary for growth and evolution.

- **Ra and Thoth**: Ra provides the energy and potential, while Thoth translates it into knowledge and understanding. Thoth's wisdom is a reflection of Ra's light, bringing clarity and insight into the nature of existence. Through Thoth, Ra's intentions are interpreted and communicated to all levels of consciousness. Thoth is the manifestation of Ra's mind, the divine intellect that seeks to understand the world created by Ra. This relationship emphasizes the need for both creativity (Ra) and comprehension (Thoth) in achieving spiritual fulfillment.

- **Thoth and Ma'at**: Thoth, as the embodiment of divine intellect, applies the laws of Ma'at in a way that makes them accessible and applicable. Thoth's wisdom ensures that the principles of Ma'at are not only understood but also implemented in ways that promote growth and enlightenment. In other words, Thoth serves as the mediator who brings Ma'at's abstract principles into the realm of human experience. Ma'at's laws are the framework, and Thoth provides the means to live within that framework through the cultivation of wisdom and moral discernment.

The Trinity in the Context of the 42 Laws of Ma'at

The 42 Laws of Ma'at encapsulate the harmonious interplay of these three divine aspects, each reinforcing the essence of the others:

- **Embodying Ra's Order**: The laws encourage individuals to live in alignment with Ra's creative order by maintaining purity, balance, and respect for all life. Through acts that honor the divine source, individuals reflect the light of Ra in their actions.

- **Applying Thoth's Wisdom**: The laws guide us to seek understanding, to live with intention, and to embrace the pursuit of knowledge. Thoth's influence in the laws is evident in their call for self-reflection, integrity, and the cultivation of the mind. By following Thoth's path, we align our thoughts and actions with the wisdom that supports Ma'at's principles.

- **Living Ma'at's Truth**: Ultimately, the laws of Ma'at provide a path for living in truth and righteousness. They are the standards by which one's soul is measured, reflecting Ma'at's role as the eternal judge. Each law represents an aspect of Ma'at's cosmic order, guiding individuals to live lives of harmony, justice, and balance.

In unison, Ra, Thoth, and Ma'at create a comprehensive vision of the divine path. Ra provides the source of life and order; Thoth offers the means to understand and interpret that order; and Ma'at ensures that it is sustained and balanced. Together, they form the foundation upon which the 42 Laws of Wisdom are built, embodying the divine principles that lead us to live in harmony with the universe. By embracing these laws, we honor Ra's light, Thoth's wisdom, and Ma'at's truth, achieving spiritual fulfillment through alignment with the divine trinity.

Chapter 1: The Law of Virtue

To be virtuous is to commit to living by principles that purify and elevate our spiritual nature. As the first Law in the **42 Laws of Wisdom**, the principle of virtue lays the foundation for a life rooted in integrity, righteousness, and truth. The 42 Laws, which represent core virtues, serve as a guide for living in harmony with the divine order and balancing both our internal and external worlds. Virtue is not simply a set of moral rules; it is a way of being that aligns us with the path of spiritual growth, enabling us to become representations of truth on all planes of manifestation.

Proverbs 4:23 instructs us to *"Guard your heart with all diligence, for out of it spring the issues of life."* Virtue, then, is a reflection of the heart's purity, guiding our actions, thoughts, and relationships with others. **Proverbs 21:21** further proclaims, *"Whoever pursues righteousness and love finds life, prosperity, and honor."* Honoring virtue, therefore, leads to a life rich in blessings, prosperity, and divine favor. **Proverbs 10:7** adds, *"The memory of the righteous is a blessing, but the name of the wicked will rot."* This highlights the enduring value of virtue, showing that the legacy of a virtuous life brings honor and blessings far beyond material wealth.

True wealth comes from divine favor, and those who live virtuously are the true recipients of spiritual and lasting abundance. By embodying virtue in ourselves, we align with divine principles that bring a life of dignity and purpose. Living with virtue means walking with truth, justice, and fairness, all of which are key principles of Ma'at.

2 Peter 1:4-5 emphasizes the importance of virtue, stating, *"Through these He has given us His very great and precious promises, so that through them you may participate in the divine nature, having escaped the corruption in the world caused by evil desires. For this very reason, make every effort to supplement your faith with virtue, and virtue with knowledge."* These verses underscore the significance of honoring virtue as a reflection of our connection to the divine nature. Because we are invited to escape worldly corruption and participate in the divine, we are called to actively pursue virtue. Virtue is not just a passive quality but a necessary foundation for spiritual growth. By cultivating virtue, we honor the sacred within ourselves and align with the divine order, fulfilling our role as righteous representatives of creation.

Metaphysically, virtue is more than a set of moral principles; it is a dynamic force that aligns the soul with the natural order of the universe. Virtues are like the pillars of divine order, supporting the structure of existence by resonating with higher frequencies. They serve as active representatives of Ma'at, reinforcing harmony, balance, and interconnectedness in the cosmos. Each virtue acts as a foundational element, channeling both individual and collective energy to sustain the architecture of divine reality. When we embody these virtues, we tap into the cosmic framework that upholds universal law, allowing us to live in alignment with the sacred principles that govern creation.

As we practice virtues like humility, truth, and compassion, we cleanse the subtle energy fields around us, releasing attachments to fear, greed, and dishonor. This clearing opens a pathway for higher wisdom to enter our consciousness, creating a space where the soul can flourish in alignment with divine principles. Virtue refines the energy of the soul, enabling it to vibrate at a frequency that harmonizes with the universal flow.

When embodying virtue, we create a ripple effect throughout our being. This purification process impacts not only our own consciousness but the energies we interact with. Virtue, in this sense, becomes the force that restores balance within ourselves and the greater world, encouraging harmony and peace.

At a metaphysical level, virtue serves as the energetic bridge that connects us to the greater wisdom of the universe. It is through living virtuously that we unlock deeper understanding and align with the natural rhythms of life. Each virtuous act reinforces our connection to the divine flow, allowing us to live in a state of inner clarity and purpose.

Philosophically, the pursuit of virtue is a process of aligning oneself with Ma'at—the cosmic order that governs both the seen and unseen realms. Virtue is not only a personal endeavor but a reflection of one's connection to the harmonious flow of the universe.

The heart, in Kemetic philosophy, is the seat of consciousness and morality. Virtue is seen as the alignment of one's heart with Ma'at, ensuring that our actions, thoughts, and words are in harmony with the divine order. To live virtuously is to live in balance, where personal integrity and social responsibility merge.

The purity of one's heart is crucial, as it is said that after death, the heart is weighed against the feather of Ma'at. A heart that is light—free from selfishness, deceit, and injustice—ensures passage into the eternal realms. Thus, virtue is not just about individual actions but about maintaining harmony with others and the natural world, reflecting a deep understanding of interconnection.

By embodying virtue, we maintain our own inner balance and contribute to the balance of the cosmos. In this way, virtue becomes a path to wisdom, as it encourages clarity of thought, purity of heart, and righteous conduct, ensuring that we are aligned with the timeless principles that sustain both the soul and the universe.

Chapter 2: The Law of Gratitude

Gratitude is more than a feeling; it is a conscious acknowledgment of the Creator's gifts—our health, our surroundings, and our very existence. The principle of Ma'at, as it relates to gratitude, teaches us that gratitude is an active practice—an acknowledgment that everything we experience is a manifestation of divine providence, the rising of the sun to the breath we take, each moment is a blessing that calls for our appreciation.

The Book of Proverbs weaves gratitude into the essence of wisdom. **Proverbs 3:9-10** reminds us to *honor the Creator with the first fruits of our labor*, recognizing that all abundance flows from a higher source. When we align with this truth, we open ourselves to receive even more blessings. **Proverbs 15:16** adds, *"Better is a little with the fear of the Lord than great treasure with trouble."* This shows us that gratitude is not about the quantity of what we possess, but the quality of our recognition of it. Through gratitude, even the simplest things become treasures, and the perception of lack dissolves into an awareness of divine sufficiency.

1 Thessalonians 5:18 – *"Give thanks in all circumstances; for this is God's will."*

This verse beautifully emphasizes the practice of gratitude in all aspects of life, reflecting the understanding that gratitude allows us to align with the divine will. Much like the teachings of Ma'at, where gratitude elevates our connection to the sacred and brings balance to our lives, this verse reminds us of the spiritual importance of maintaining a thankful heart, regardless of external circumstances. When we express gratitude, we recognize that God's will flows from a standpoint of giving, and as appreciative recipients, we magnify and intensify the blessings we receive. In this way, gratitude becomes a key to unlocking greater abundance and harmony.

Metaphysically, gratitude is a transformative state of being that elevates both the mind and the spirit. Gratitude shifts the vibrational frequency of the individual, raising consciousness to higher realms where abundance and harmony naturally reside. When we embody gratitude, we open the channels of divine energy, allowing it to flow freely through us and uplift our entire energetic field.

Gratitude is more than an emotional response—it is an energetic exchange. Each time we express sincere thanks, we activate a higher frequency within ourselves, aligning with the universal flow of creation. This alignment brings us into resonance with the energy of abundance, unlocking the pathways through which blessings can manifest in our lives. On a higher level, gratitude is a force that goes beyond the material plane, enabling the individual to attract not only material abundance but also spiritual enlightenment. It refines the spirit and purifies the mind, freeing us from lower vibrations of lack, fear, and dissatisfaction.

In this elevated state, the mind becomes more attuned to divine wisdom, and the spirit becomes more receptive to higher truths. Gratitude acts as a harmonizer, balancing the energies within and around us, creating an aura of peace, fulfillment, and joy. By cultivating gratitude, we transform our reality, allowing us to partake fully in the gifts of the universe, both seen and unseen. Through this law, we become active participants in the cosmic dance, recognizing that the more we appreciate, the more we receive.

Philosophically, gratitude is more than a feeling; it is a powerful state of alignment with the laws of the universe. In ancient wisdom traditions, gratitude is seen as a key to maintaining balance within oneself and with the cosmos. When we express gratitude, we acknowledge the abundance and interconnectedness of all life. This recognition opens us to the flow of divine energy and allows us to magnetize more of what we need. Gratitude, then, is not passive; it is an active force that harmonizes us with the natural order, making us more receptive to the gifts of life.

Gratitude aligns with the law of correspondence, which teaches that the harmony we create within mirrors the harmony we experience without. As we express gratitude, we invoke the law of attraction, drawing more opportunities for growth, abundance, and fulfillment into our lives. By humbling ourselves in acknowledgment of the Creator's gifts, we affirm our connection to the universal flow, recognizing that life is a continuous exchange of energy. This law teaches that gratitude is the bridge that connects us to the higher frequencies of existence, enabling us to rise above the limitations of the material world.

Chapter 3: The Law of Peace

In the sacred law of Ma'at, the *Law of Peace* embodies harmony within oneself and with the world around us. Peace is not simply the absence of conflict; it requires a conscious choice to live in alignment with the natural order of the universe. It is the cultivation of inner balance, a foundation from which we navigate life with clarity and grace. When we embody peace, we create a space of serenity that radiates outward, influencing both our internal world and the environment around us.

Proverbs 14:30 reminds us, *"A heart at peace gives life to the body, but envy rots the bones."* This reflects the vital connection between peace and well-being. Peace has the power to heal, restore vitality, and promote spiritual and physical health. When we cultivate peace within, we align with divine rhythms that dissolve internal and external conflict, creating harmony in our surroundings.

It is through peace that we contribute to the balance of the cosmos and align ourselves with the divine rhythms of the universe. Choosing peace is an act of love, compassion, and understanding, ensuring that our presence brings harmony rather than turmoil.

Isaiah 26:3 further emphasizes this: *"You will keep in perfect peace all who trust in You, all whose thoughts are fixed on You!"* This verse underscores that when one's mind is focused on the Creator, they are infused with truth, which brings deep peace to the spirit. By trusting in truth, righteousness, and living according to divine principles—embodied in Ma'at—peace naturally follows. This internal peace becomes a reflection of the mind's alignment with divine truth, allowing us to remain calm and balanced in all circumstances.

Metaphysically, peace does not equate to the lack of problems or issues, but rather represents a profound inner ability to maintain resilience regardless of the situation. Peace is a vibrational frequency that nurtures the soul and sustains both spiritual and physical well-being. When we embody peace, we create a protective energetic field that shields us from external negativity and disharmony. This inner peace is a source of vitality, a key to longevity and healing, as it allows the mind and body to operate in a state of coherence with the divine order.

Peace elevates consciousness, enabling us to rise above the distractions and chaos of the material world. It promotes clarity of thought and emotional equilibrium, making us more receptive to the guidance of the higher self. By cultivating inner peace, we align ourselves with the natural flow of the universe, creating a space where healing, growth, and transformation can flourish. In this state, we are no longer influenced by the lower vibrations of fear, anger, or envy, but are anchored in the steady current of divine serenity.

Philosophically, peace is the recognition of the interconnectedness of all things. In ancient wisdom traditions, it is understood that conflict arises from the illusion of separation, while peace comes from the understanding that all things are part of a greater whole. Peace is not passive; it is an active engagement with the world from a place of inner harmony and balance. When we are peaceful, we are in alignment with the cosmic order, understanding that everything has its place and purpose in the universe.

Peace is also a reflection of wisdom. The wise understand that true power does not come from domination or control, but from the ability to remain centered and calm in the face of life's challenges. By promoting peace, we cultivate joy and contentment, as we no longer seek validation from external sources but find fulfillment in our alignment with universal truth. Peace allows us to act with love, compassion, and understanding, creating a ripple effect that cultivates harmony in our relationships and the world around us.

To live in peace is to acknowledge that the external world is a reflection of our internal state. When we embody the ***Law of Peace***, we not only create balance within ourselves but contribute to the balance and harmony of the entire cosmos. Peace is the foundation of spiritual growth and enlightenment, as it allows us to move through life with grace and clarity, unshaken by the turbulence of the material world.

Chapter 4: The Law of Respect

The *Law of Respect* is a fundamental aspect of Ma'at's teachings, emphasizing the importance of honoring personal boundaries, whether they are physical, emotional, or spiritual. In this chapter, we explore the law of respect through the angle of respecting the property of others, as this is one of the most common forms of disrespect observed in society. Respecting the property of others is not merely about avoiding theft or dishonesty; it is a recognition of the sacred connection between individuals and their energy, effort, and personal space. In doing so, we maintain the natural balance of the universe and contribute to harmony and justice.

Romans 13:7 advises, *"Pay to all what is owed to them: taxes to whom taxes are owed, revenue to whom revenue is owed, respect to whom respect is owed, honor to whom honor is owed."* This scripture supports the idea that respect and honor are due where they are deserved, underscoring the Law of Respect as an obligation to maintain harmony within divine order. **Proverbs 22:22-23** further reminds us, *"Do not rob the poor because they are poor, or crush the afflicted at the gate, for the Lord will plead their cause and will plunder the soul of those who plunder them."* Respecting others—especially those who may be vulnerable—ensures that we align with universal justice, reinforcing trust and equity in our interactions.

Metaphysically, the property and space of others represent extensions of their energy and intention. By respecting what belongs to others, we acknowledge and respect the energetic attachments they may have formed. Disrespecting these boundaries disrupts the natural flow of harmony, pushing us toward the negative end of the polarity spectrum and potentially leading to conflict, discord, or further imbalance. Respecting others' property aligns us with higher principles of cosmic justice and balance, bringing our actions into harmony with universal laws. This respect strengthens our spiritual integrity, as honoring the property of others mirrors the reverence we hold for greater forces of harmony and justice.

Philosophically, respect within the principles of Ma'at reflects the virtues of humility, empathy, and accountability. It is not rooted in fear or submission but is a genuine acknowledgment of divine order that manifests in the world around us. Respecting the boundaries and property of others aligns us with a cycle of reciprocity and balance, sustaining trust within the broader cosmic network. Additionally, respect is a form of awareness that calls us to recognize the strength, knowledge, and attributes in others, inspiring us to cultivate these qualities within ourselves. By acknowledging the abilities of others, we are motivated to rise to our highest potential, cultivating a harmonious community that encourages collective growth.

Respect also aligns with a mindset of abundance and prosperity. By honoring the efforts, possessions, and spaces of others, we demonstrate trust in the universe's capacity to provide. This moves us away from *unhealthy* competition and toward cooperation, reinforcing the idea that resources flow through divine order. As we honor what belongs to others, we strengthen our alignment with abundance, harmonizing with the forces of fairness and the universal flow of prosperity.

To live by the ***Law of Respect*** is to cultivate a mindset of reverence, empathy, and understanding. By respecting others' property and personal space, we build trust and create a community rooted in shared dignity, where each individual can freely express themselves and contribute to the collective good. Respect thus becomes the foundation of meaningful connections, enabling each of us to thrive in an environment of mutual honor and support.

Chapter 5: The Law of the Sacredness of Life

The ancient principle of Ma'at, now expressed as the ***Law of the Sacredness of Life***, calls us to recognize the divine craftsmanship in all creation. Every living form, every creature, is a testament to the wisdom and purpose of the Creator. By honoring the sacredness of life, we acknowledge the divine energy that flows through all things, understanding that each life is a reflection of the divine order.

Proverbs 3:19-20 reminds us, *"By wisdom the Lord laid the earth's foundations, by understanding He set the heavens in place; by His knowledge the watery depths were divided, and the clouds let drop the dew."* This verse highlights the profound wisdom with which the Creator established the universe, underscoring the sacredness of all life as part of that divine blueprint.

Proverbs 8:35 further states, *"For whoever finds me finds life and receives favor from the Lord."* When one approaches life with this law in mind, they behold creation through the lens of the divine presence in all things. Since God is both the Creator and creation, to look upon creation is to find the life-giving essence of God in all forms. By seeing God in all life, one affirms its sacredness and, in doing so, receives divine favor. This understanding of life's sanctity elevates our connection to the divine and deepens our reverence for the interconnectedness of all existence.

Colossians 1:16 states, *"For by him all things were created: things in heaven and on earth, visible and invisible, whether thrones or powers or rulers or authorities; all things were created through him and for him."* This verse powerfully aligns with the principle of Ma'at, affirming the sacredness of all life. It emphasizes that everything in existence, both seen and unseen, was created by the divine and reflects God's presence. This understanding reinforces the idea that every form of life carries sacred value, and as such, must be honored and protected.

Metaphysically, the affirmation of life's sacredness expands our consciousness beyond the material plane. By viewing all life as sacred, we align ourselves with the divine blueprint that flows through all creation. Life is a manifestation of the divine essence that permeates the cosmos. Every living being carries within it the spark of divine energy, and when we recognize this, we move beyond the limitations of ordinary perception.

The sacredness of life is not limited to human experience; it encompasses all forms of existence—plants, animals, the elements, and even the unseen forces of nature. By affirming this law, we tap into the interconnectedness of all things and align ourselves with the higher order of the universe. The energy we send out—whether through our thoughts, words, or actions—creates ripples in the cosmic web, affecting not only ourselves but the larger collective. Through this, we become active participants in the preservation and nourishment of life's sacred flow, contributing to the eternal harmony of the cosmos.

Philosophically, to affirm that all life is sacred is to acknowledge the intrinsic value of all living beings. In the tradition of Ma'at, life is viewed as a delicate balance sustained by principles of truth, justice, and righteousness. The reverence for life is an act of aligning oneself with this balance, recognizing that no life is insignificant. Every creature, every element of nature, has a purpose within the grand design of the universe.

From a philosophical standpoint, respecting the sacredness of life means understanding that our role is not to dominate or exploit creation but to live in harmony with it. To honor life is to honor the divine order that maintains equilibrium in the natural world. This understanding leads us to live with compassion, mindfulness, and responsibility, knowing that the way we treat life directly impacts the overall harmony of existence. In ancient thought, the wise individual does not simply exist but thrives by cultivating a deep respect for the life force that sustains the universe, thus preserving the balance and ensuring personal and collective peace.

Chapter 6: The Law of Genuine Offerings

To give genuine offerings is to offer from the heart, with purity and sincerity. ***The Law of Genuine Offerings*** speaks to the deep spiritual truth that our offerings are not measured by their size or value, but by the intention behind them.

Proverbs 21:3 echoes this law: *"To do what is right and just is more acceptable to the Lord than sacrifice."* This teaches that the heart behind the offering is what matters most. A genuine offering reflects our respect for the divine and our desire to be on the right side of manifestation, aligning ourselves with the Creator, who constantly offers genuine gifts in the form of life, abundance, and the natural order. In giving sincerely, we mirror the divine act of creation, participating in the flow of blessings.

2 Corinthians 9:7 – *"Each one must give as he has decided in his heart, not reluctantly or under compulsion, for God loves a cheerful giver."* This verse emphasizes the importance of giving from the heart, aligning perfectly with the principle of Ma'at that offerings must be genuine and sincere. True offerings, whether material or spiritual, are given freely and with joy, symbolizing the purity of the giver's spirit and their connection to divine principles.

Metaphysically, giving genuine offerings is about energy exchange. It is not merely the act of giving but the vibrational frequency that accompanies the offering. When we give with sincerity and truth, we transmit positive energy into the universe. The offering, whether material or immaterial, becomes a symbol of our alignment with the divine flow of abundance. Through this energy exchange, the giver opens themselves to receive blessings in return, creating a harmonious cycle of giving and receiving.

Genuine offerings are a reflection of the purity of intent. When our heart and mind are aligned with the act of giving, the energy we put out nourishes both the giver and the receiver. It contributes to the overall harmony of the universe, ensuring that what we offer resonates with truth, love, and the desire to uplift others. This metaphysical act of offering is a manifestation of our connection to the higher principles of balance and reciprocity.

Philosophically, the act of giving has long been understood as a sacred exchange that upholds the balance between the individual and the collective. It is rooted in the belief that the material world is interconnected with spiritual truths, and offerings are a way of participating in that divine order. The sincerity of an offering lies not only in its intention but in the awareness that it contributes to the broader harmony of existence. When offerings are given with humility and compassion, they sustain this equilibrium, honoring the interconnected nature of life.

The act of giving is a reflection of the internal harmony one maintains with the natural order. Offerings serve as a bridge between the material and the spiritual, ensuring that the flow of abundance is cyclical and that we remain in tune with the forces that sustain creation. Through genuine offerings, we align ourselves with these eternal principles, promoting growth not just for ourselves but for the world around us.

When offerings are made with sincerity and of the highest value, they can enhance even our personal relationships, including successful business dealings. Genuine offerings, whether in the form of time, resources, or intentions, build trust and mutual respect. In both personal and business interactions, the authenticity of these exchanges creates a foundation for success, promoting harmony and cooperation. When we give from a place of truth and respect, our relationships—whether personal or professional—thrive.

Chapter 7: The Law of Truth

Living in truth means shaping ourselves after the highest attributes and virtues, aligning our lives with principles that reflect integrity, righteousness, and divine wisdom. ***The Law of Truth*** extends beyond simple honesty; it calls for embodying truth in every facet of life—through our actions, thoughts, and intentions. Truth is the cornerstone of integrity, a value deeply rooted in both Ma'at and the teachings of wisdom.

Proverbs 12:19 reminds us, *"Truthful lips endure forever, but a lying tongue lasts only a moment."* This verse highlights the eternal nature of truth, in contrast to the fleeting nature of falsehood. Truth is unwavering and stable, a guiding force that aligns us with the cosmic law. To live in truth is to live in harmony with the divine, where our words and deeds reflect the purity of our soul and our commitment to authenticity.

Building on this, **John 8:32** reveals another dimension of truth's power: *"Then you will know the truth, and the truth will set you free."* Here, truth is not just a moral ideal but a liberating force, one that breaks the chains of ignorance and darkness. Truth, in this context, is a spiritual key that sets us free from the bondage imposed by external forces, societal conditioning, or even self-deception. It liberates us from the limitations of falsehood, allowing us to see clearly the path toward spiritual enlightenment.

When we live in truth, we free ourselves from the illusions created by fear, manipulation, or ignorance. Truth becomes the light that dispels the darkness, revealing the divine order in all things. It empowers us to act from a place of integrity and wisdom, leading us toward spiritual clarity and growth. By living in truth, we not only align with the cosmic order but also safeguard ourselves from the bondage imposed by entities—whether deliberate or unaware—who seek to lead us astray.

Metaphysically, truth is synonymous with the divine. Living in truth is living in alignment with the essence of creation itself, as truth and God are not separate but one and the same. To live in truth means to embody divine principles in every aspect of our existence, aligning our actions, thoughts, and intentions with higher wisdom. It is through truth that we gain clarity and understanding, stripping away the illusions of the material world. Living in truth requires the courage to face reality as it is, knowing that only through truth can we access genuine wisdom, transformation, and spiritual evolution. When we live truthfully, we live in accordance with divine order, allowing us to fully embrace our soul's purpose.

Philosophically, living in truth is a pathway to enlightenment. In ancient wisdom traditions, truth is considered a sacred treasure, a key to unlocking higher consciousness. To live in truth is to live in alignment with universal laws, where truth is seen not only as intellectual knowledge but as a way of being that harmonizes with the natural order. Truth is the guiding force that shapes integrity, honor, and justice. It is not merely about avoiding falsehood but about striving to live authentically in every moment, reflecting the highest virtues. Living in truth requires self-discipline and the constant pursuit of wisdom, clarity, and insight, as it allows individuals to rise above the ordinary and connect with the divine.

Chapter 8: The Law of Reverence for Altars

The Law of Reverence for Altars calls us to honor the sacred spaces where the divine and the material meet. Altars, whether physical or spiritual, represent a point of connection between humanity and the higher realms. In Ma'at's wisdom, respecting altars symbolizes reverence for the divine presence in all things, recognizing that the sacred is everywhere.

Proverbs 24:3-4 offers, *"By wisdom a house is built, and through understanding it is established; through knowledge its rooms are filled with rare and beautiful treasures."* This reflects the idea that sacred spaces are created through wisdom and reverence, and when respected, they become places filled with spiritual treasures and divine presence. This is why all sacred spaces must be respected, as they are deliberate attempts to concentrate divine energy, aligned with the spiritual intentions of those who create and maintain these altars. Each altar reflects the energy signatures of its creators, and by revering these spaces, we honor not only the individuals' efforts to connect with the divine but also the sacred flow of energy that nourishes the space, making it a place of spiritual refuge and power. There is no god or set of gods greater than another, as the "gods" are humanity's attempt to identify the infinite aspects of the one Creator.

Metaphysically, altars represent more than physical objects; they are focal points where spiritual energy and intention converge. Altars serve as portals to higher realms, spaces where the divine and the material intersect. By respecting altars, we honor the delicate balance between the visible and invisible worlds. When we approach these sacred spaces with reverence, we acknowledge the spiritual energy present and contribute to its amplification. Every offering made at an altar —whether material or immaterial—is an exchange of energy, a way of aligning ourselves with the divine flow. Metaphysically, the respect for altars is a practice of acknowledging the unseen forces that support and sustain life. Through this respect, we maintain the integrity of sacred spaces and reinforce our connection to the divine currents that flow through them.

Furthermore, altars serve as mirrors of our inner sanctity. The way we treat these spaces reflects how we respect our own spiritual path and energy. By maintaining the sanctity of altars, we also maintain the sanctity of our spiritual practice. When we honor altars, we cultivate a deep awareness of the divine forces that reside not only in these spaces but also within ourselves.

Philosophically, respecting altars aligns with ancient teachings about the sacredness of life and the interconnectedness of all things. Altars symbolize the bridge between the spiritual and the physical, and by treating these spaces with reverence, we honor the natural order. This respect is a reflection of our understanding that the divine resides in all things, and that sacred spaces act as concentrated points of divine energy. The recognition of this energy in altars is an extension of the principle that all life and all spaces can be sanctified when treated with reverence.

In this way, respecting altars also reflects the idea that boundaries, both physical and spiritual, are important to maintaining balance in the universe. Just as boundaries between individuals maintain harmony in relationships, the boundaries between the material and the spiritual realms maintain cosmic balance. Altars act as gateways that mark these boundaries, and by respecting them, we honor the balance between the earthly and the divine.

Chapter 9: The Law of Sincerity

To speak with sincerity is to channel words that carry the power of truth, wisdom, and compassion. ***The Law of Sincerity*** guides us to ensure that our deeds and every word we utter reflects our inner integrity and aligns with our higher self. Sincere words are not only truthful but spoken with the intention to uplift, enlighten, and benefit others. **Proverbs 18:21** teaches, *"The tongue has the power of life and death, and those who love it will eat its fruit."* This reminds us that our words hold the potential to create or destroy, to heal or to harm.

Speaking with sincerity means embracing the responsibility of our words, ensuring that they are rooted in love and honesty. When we speak with sincerity, our words become instruments of transformation, carrying the force of truth and creating positive shifts in those we communicate with.

Metaphysically, sincerity aligns our words with the vibrational frequency of authenticity and integrity. Speech is not merely a communication tool, but an extension of our soul's energy, resonating beyond the material plane. Words carry power, and when they are spoken with sincerity, they create harmonious ripples in the energetic field, reinforcing our connection to higher truths. Sincere words are imbued with the force of creation, shaping reality in alignment with divine order. When we speak from a place of truth, our energy is clear, allowing us to manifest relationships and experiences that reflect trust, clarity, and spiritual growth.

Philosophically, sincerity is not just the practice of truth-telling but the embodiment of harmony between our thoughts, beliefs, and spoken words. In ancient wisdom traditions, the spoken word is considered a creative force, and the alignment of one's speech with sincerity ensures that our words resonate with purpose and intention. Speaking with sincerity invokes the law of correspondence, where the harmony within is reflected in the harmony of the external world. When our words match our intentions, we create balance, enabling our thoughts to manifest powerfully and authentically. Through sincere speech, we engage the law of vibration, ensuring that what we speak resonates at a frequency of love, truth, and purpose, contributing to the upliftment and evolution of both ourselves and those we communicate with.

Chapter 10: The Law of Moderation

The Law of Moderation teaches us to consume only our fair share, aligning ourselves with the natural law of abundance and balance. It is a recognition that the universe provides for all who trust in its flow, and that greed or overconsumption arises from a misconception of lack. In truth, abundance is the natural state of the universe. The idea that resources are limited is an illusion—a construct born from fear, control, and the imbalance caused by selfish accumulation.

Poverty itself is not a natural state but a product of this misalignment with divine principles. When we recognize the abundance around us and consume only what we need, we honor the universal flow and ensure that others too can access their share. We must not only ensure our own consumption remains balanced, but also take responsibility for facilitating abundance in the lives of others—mentally, energetically, and physically. When we consume fairly, we affirm that the universe provides enough for everyone, and we commit to sharing that abundance with those in our circle of influence.

2 Corinthians 9:8 states, *"And God is able to bless you abundantly, so that in all things at all times, having all that you need, you will abound in every good work."* This verse emphasizes that divine provision is ever-present, and that greed is unnecessary. When we take only what we need and share with others, we acknowledge that abundance flows naturally and that everyone has enough. The principle of moderation aligns with Ma'at's wisdom of balance, fairness, and equity. It also underscores the importance of maintaining harmony between what we take and what we offer, recognizing that life is a constant exchange of energy and resources.

Metaphysically, consuming only one's fair share maintains the balance of energy in the universe. Overconsumption distorts the natural flow of abundance, creating blockages not just in the material world but in the energetic realm as well. By taking only what we need, we keep the channels of abundance open for ourselves and others, contributing to a cycle of continuous flow and prosperity. Consumption in moderation keeps us attuned to the natural rhythm of the cosmos, ensuring that we live in harmony with universal laws and principles of reciprocity.

Philosophically, this law calls upon ancient wisdom that emphasizes discipline, self-control, and the idea that there is enough for all when resources are used with respect and awareness. The perception of scarcity is born from a misunderstanding of the universe's abundant nature. When we consume only what is necessary, we act in alignment with principles of fairness, justice, and mutual respect. This balance ensures the well-being of the whole community and reflects our understanding that the earth's resources are meant to sustain all living beings, not just the few.

Chapter 11: The Law of Good Intention

The *Law of Good Intention* is a profound principle rooted in the understanding that our thoughts, emotions, and actions are imbued with energy that shapes the world around us. In the teachings of Ma'at, intention is sacred, reflecting the divine order and harmony of the universe. When we act with clarity of purpose and love, we infuse our deeds with the weight of truth, ensuring that every thought, word, and action aligns with the highest good. Each intention is recorded by the scribes of creation into the Hall of Records, adding subatomic weight to our hearts, which will one day be weighed against the feather of Ma'at. Thus, the essence of this law lies in recognizing the power of our intentions as transformative forces for ourselves and others.

The biblical verse from **Proverbs 16:2** states, *"All one's ways may be pure in one's own eyes, but the LORD weighs the spirit."* This scripture emphasizes that while our intentions may appear righteous, it is the purity of our motives that ultimately matters. The divine sees beyond surface actions, probing the depths of our hearts to discern our true intentions. When we align our actions with good intentions, we mirror the wisdom of Ma'at, promoting balance and integrity in our lives and the lives of those around us.

Metaphysically, the *Law of Good Intention* emphasizes the vibrational frequency of our thoughts and emotions. Every intention carries an energetic signature that impacts our reality. When we cultivate clarity in our minds' eye and focus our energy on positive outcomes, we become co-creators of our experience. This intentional focus acts as a magnet, attracting experiences that resonate with our desires. Understanding that each intention holds the power to shape our reality invites us to be more mindful and conscious in our thought processes.

The vibrational quality of our intentions can be compared to the principle of resonance. Just as tuning forks vibrate at specific frequencies, our intentions send out ripples that influence the energy around us. Intentions rooted in love, compassion, and understanding create harmonious vibrations, promoting connections and positive transformations. Conversely, intentions steeped in negativity or fear can lead to dissonance, disrupting the flow of energy in our lives. Thus, cultivating good intentions is essential for manifesting a reality aligned with the universal truth.

Philosophically, the *Law of Good Intention* aligns closely with ancient teachings, particularly the principle of correspondence, which states, "As above, so below; as within, so without." Our internal states of being directly influence our external experiences. By nurturing good intentions within ourselves, we can create a ripple effect that resonates outward, creating harmony and balance in our interactions with the world. This principle echoes teachings that highlight the interconnectedness of all life and the importance of aligning our thoughts and actions with divine principles.

Additionally, this law relates to the alchemical process of transformation. Just as alchemists sought to turn base metals into gold, our intentions can transmute ordinary experiences into profound insights and growth. When we approach our lives with intention, we become the alchemists of our reality, transforming challenges into opportunities for wisdom and enlightenment. Speaking, acting, and thinking with good intent allows us to channel the transformative energy of the universe, creating a life of purpose and meaning.

To embody the *Law of Good Intention* is to awaken to the sacred power of our thoughts, emotions, and actions. As we strive to align our intentions with the principles of Ma'at, we engage in a spiritual practice that enriches our lives and the lives of those around us. By consciously choosing to act from a place of love and clarity, we contribute to the creation of a harmonious reality that reflects the divine order of the universe. Let us embrace the responsibility of our intentions, recognizing that each thought and action adds weight to our hearts and shapes the world in which we live. In doing so, we become catalysts for healing, connection, and wisdom, weaving a fabric of love that resonates through all of existence.

Chapter 12: The Law of Peaceful Relations

Relating in peace is a mark of spiritual maturity, reflecting the depth of one's inner stability and alignment with divine harmony. *The law of Peaceful Relations* let us emphasize, is not about naively ignoring the challenges of the world, nor is it a passive state. Instead, it is an intentional and active approach to engaging with life, grounded in wisdom and understanding. It is about embodying the calm, balanced energy of a wise spirit—one who seeks the truth in every aspect of life. To relate in peace is to walk in harmony with oneself and others, allowing the universe and energetic spaces to complement and elevate your presence wherever you go. In doing so, you become a representative of peace, influencing your surroundings and creating ripples of tranquility.

Romans 12:18 states, *"If it is possible, as far as it depends on you, live at peace with everyone."* This verse highlights the conscious responsibility we carry in maintaining peace in our relationships. It aligns with the principle of relating in peace, encouraging us to actively seek harmony, regardless of external circumstances. Peace is not something passively received but an intentional state we create through our thoughts, actions, and energies.

Metaphysically, peace is not merely the absence of discord but a natural byproduct of harmony and understanding. When true balance is achieved within, peace emerges as the reflection of that inner alignment. To relate in peace is to engage with the world from a place of internal equilibrium, where the vibrations of anger, jealousy, or conflict are dissolved. When we embody peace, we carry an aura of tranquility that influences not only our immediate environment but also the broader energetic field around us.

By choosing to relate in peace, we align our personal energy with the universal flow, creating a harmonious resonance between ourselves and the cosmos. This principle teaches that peace is an active force that goes beyond individual interactions, helping to raise the vibrational frequency of entire spaces. In this state, even challenging or hostile environments are transformed into places of healing and growth. When we are at peace within, the universe mirrors that peace back to us in our interactions with others.

Philosophically, relating in peace is an act of wisdom and spiritual maturity. Ancient teachings emphasize that true peace in relationships is built on the virtues of patience, humility, and understanding. These qualities form the foundation of peaceful interactions because they allow us to approach others with empathy and compassion, even in moments of tension. Relating in peace means recognizing that every person, every situation, is an opportunity to reflect the divine nature within ourselves.

By embracing peaceful interactions, we embody the principles of balance and reciprocity, recognizing that every word and action sends ripples through the interconnected web of existence. To live in peace is to reject the illusions of separation and conflict, choosing instead to act as a unifying force in the world. In doing so, we affirm the sacredness of all beings and the importance of harmony as the foundation of meaningful relationships.

To live by ***The Law of Peaceful Relations*** is to embrace a life of balance and unity. It is a commitment to creating peaceful connections with all beings and contributing to the harmony of the world. Through peace, we walk the path of Ma'at, living with grace, wisdom, and an unwavering commitment to unity and love.

Chapter 13: The Law of Reverence for Animal Life

To live by the ***Law of Reverence for Animal Life*** is to recognize animals' role in the intricate balance of life. This law teaches that animals, while different from humans, hold significant value in the natural world. They are manifestations of divine wisdom, offering guidance, resources, and lessons that contribute to our survival and spiritual growth. Animals often act as signposts in nature, pointing us to essential resources like water, plants, and shelter, and they embody qualities such as patience, loyalty, and strength.

Genesis 1:26 states, *"Then God said, 'Let us make mankind in our image, in our likeness, so that they may rule over the fish in the sea and the birds in the sky, over the livestock and all the wild animals, and over all the creatures that move along the ground.'"* While this verse speaks of dominion, it implies responsibility and stewardship—entrusting humans with the care and respect for animals, recognizing them as part of divine creation, each playing a unique role in the broader ecosystem.

Metaphysically, animals serve as reflections of divine order within nature. They are not equal to humans in consciousness but represent an essential aspect of the balance that sustains life on earth. Animals act as guides and, in many ways, teachers, their behaviors often pointing us toward important resources in the natural world, such as edible plants, water sources, or safe shelter. Living by the ***Law of Reverence for Animal Life*** means being mindful of their roles as conduits of divine wisdom, offering lessons in survival and balance that we, as humans, can learn from.

When we interact with animals, we are reminded of our interconnectedness with all living things. While animals do not operate on the same spiritual plane as humans, their presence in the ecosystem reflects the intricate design of the universe, where each creature has a purpose. Respecting animals is not about elevating them to the same level as humans but recognizing the sacredness in their existence as part of the natural order.

Philosophically, the *Law of Reverence for Animal Life* highlights virtues such as mindfulness, responsibility, and care. The ancient understanding emphasizes that animals are integral to the earth's cycles and systems, offering wisdom in their simplicity. Animals demonstrate survival skills and natural instincts that guide us toward balance and sustainability. Reverence for animals lies in recognizing their contributions to the ecosystem, their ability to point us to life-sustaining resources, and the lessons they provide in resilience, adaptability, and instinctual knowledge.

Chapter 14: The Law of Trustworthiness

Trust is the cornerstone of all relationships, both in the material world and in the spiritual realm. The ***Law of Trustworthiness*** represents the embodiment of reliability, integrity, and truthfulness. To be trusted is to be seen as a person who can uphold commitments and maintain confidences, not only in interpersonal connections but in one's spiritual relationship with the Creator. Trustworthiness is not merely about maintaining secrets but about being a faithful steward of the responsibilities and gifts bestowed upon us by the divine.

Proverbs 11:13 tells us, *"A gossip goes about telling secrets, but one who is trustworthy in spirit keeps a confidence."* This verse highlights the importance of trust in personal relationships. To be trusted is to protect what is sacred to others and to act with integrity in every aspect of life.

Luke 16:10 further adds, *"Whoever can be trusted with very little can also be trusted with much, and whoever is dishonest with very little will also be dishonest with much."* This verse reminds us that trustworthiness is a quality that grows through consistency and faithfulness in both small and great matters. It speaks to the spiritual responsibility of being "worthy" of Trust with the gifts, insight, and opportunities that the Creator provides.

Metaphysically, trustworthiness is akin to the structure of a trust, where the self-aware individual embodies the role of the trustee. In this analogy, the Creator acts as the guarantor, facilitating the universe's energies and resources to fulfill divine will. All elements within one's environment—people, places, and things—serve as the beneficiaries of the trustee's choices and actions.

This interconnectedness emphasizes that trustworthiness not only strengthens the bond between the individual and the Divine but also enriches the collective experience.

Furthermore, trustworthiness extends beyond the material plane; it is a reflection of a soul's alignment with divine truth. To be trusted by others, and by the Creator, signifies one's readiness to receive higher spiritual gifts, such as wisdom, prophecy, or divine knowledge. Trustworthiness, in this sense, demands a deep sense of responsibility because the trusted individual becomes a custodian of sacred knowledge meant to uplift, heal, and guide others. Being worthy of divine trust means one is called to maintain their integrity not only in personal relationships but also in their spiritual duties, thus acting as a representative of divine light.

Philosophically, trustworthiness is the foundation of ethical living. Trust is a social contract between individuals, and a breach of trust undermines the very fabric of community and spiritual unity. Trustworthiness requires self-discipline, moral clarity, and the unwavering resolve to uphold truth, even when faced with personal challenges or temptations. In ancient wisdom traditions, trustworthiness was regarded as a virtue that underpinned justice, as only those who could be trusted were fit to lead or make decisions that affected the lives of others. It is through trustworthiness that societies, as well as spiritual systems, can function in harmony.

The *Law of Trustworthiness* reminds us that to be worthy of trust, we must act as reliable stewards of the divine and human trust placed upon us. It is not enough to simply avoid betrayal or dishonesty; one must actively embody the values of truth, integrity, and reliability in all aspects of life. Whether in our interpersonal relationships or in our spiritual walk, trustworthiness is a guiding principle that allows us to connect deeply with others and with the divine, ensuring that we are worthy recipients of higher knowledge, responsibilities, and opportunities.

Chapter 15: The Law of Sacred Earthkeeping

To live by the ***Law of Sacred Earthkeeping*** is to honor the divine responsibility given to humanity. This law speaks to our duty to protect and nurture the planet, recognizing that Earth is not merely a resource but a living entity—a sacred creation that sustains all life. Just as we tend to our bodies (our bodies being the metaphysical earth), we must tend to the Earth itself, ensuring that its balance and abundance remain intact for generations to come.

Genesis 2:15 states, *"The Lord God took the man and put him in the Garden of Eden to work it and take care of it."* This passage underscores the divine commission given to humanity to steward and protect the Earth. Adam's responsibility to care for the garden reflects humanity's broader responsibility to preserve and honor the planet, recognizing that the well-being of the Earth is intricately connected to the well-being of humanity.

Metaphysically, the Earth represents not only the physical world but also the energy that sustains life. The Earth emits frequencies, such as the Schumann resonances, that are essential to maintaining the balance and harmony of life on this planet. Caring for the Earth aligns us with these energetic frequencies, enhancing spiritual growth and attuning us to the divine wisdom embedded in creation.

The Earth, as a manifestation of the divine, offers us more than just physical sustenance; it provides a grounding force that stabilizes and harmonizes our spiritual energy. When we care for the Earth, we reciprocate the balance and abundance it provides, allowing us to grow spiritually and live in alignment with the cosmic order. Caring for the Earth is not just a material duty but a sacred spiritual practice, where we recognize the Earth as a living entity, part of the divine flow of life.

Philosophically, caring for the Earth reflects the ancient principle of reciprocity. In the wisdom traditions, it is understood that nature is not separate from humanity but an extension of our being. Ancient philosophies teach us that to care for the land is to respect the cycles of life, death, and rebirth that govern existence. The Earth, with its seasons and natural rhythms, mirrors the divine balance found within the soul, reminding us that everything operates in harmony when we honor our role as stewards.

The law of compensation, central to ancient wisdom traditions, teaches that what we give to the Earth, we receive in return. When we exploit or neglect the Earth, we upset this balance, resulting in scarcity and disharmony. By living in alignment with the natural order, we ensure that we maintain abundance, not just for ourselves but for all future generations. This ancient understanding emphasizes that the Earth must be treated with reverence and care, just as we would treat a precious gift from the divine.

The Earth can be seen as the university we are now attending—a sacred school or playground where we learn and grow. It provides the lessons we need for spiritual development, guiding us to evolve through our experiences here. Through our relationship with the Earth, we gain insights, develop our character, and learn to harmonize with the natural rhythms of life.

Chapter 16: The Law of Inner Wisdom

The Law of Inner Wisdom teaches the value of independent thinking, self-reliance, and the importance of cultivating inner insight. It encourages the practice of listening to one's own discernment and guidance while navigating life. While external advice from teachers and guides is important, this principle emphasizes the need to reflect deeply and develop one's own insights, aligning them with divine truth.

The verse **James 1:5** – *"If any of you lacks wisdom, let him ask of God, who gives to all generously and without reproach, and it will be given to him"* – aligns perfectly with the principle of **"Inner Wisdom."**

When we seek wisdom, it is crucial to quiet the mind, creating an internal space for divine whispers to guide us. This process emphasizes the internal work necessary to inquire deeply and receive answers from the Creator, who holds all knowledge. It's an act of both humility and strength, as we learn to rely on divine guidance through reflection and trust. Independent thought, in this context, is about redirecting how we receive insights—shifting from external sources to the still, inner voice connected to the divine.

Metaphysically, the ***Law of Inner Wisdom*** is about attuning to the inner voice that guides us on the path of truth. It involves quieting the external noise of opinions, societal expectations, and distractions, allowing us to listen to the inner wisdom that aligns with our higher purpose. Independent thinking is a reflection of spiritual maturity, as it is through inner contemplation that one connects with the universal mind and divine order.

When we cultivate inner wisdom, we create a sacred space where our thoughts and ideas can flourish, untouched by external interference. It is in this space of internal reflection that we make decisions in alignment with the higher good and divine will. By cultivating an independent mind, we ensure that our decisions and actions resonate with the truth that is unique to our own journey.

Philosophically, this law reflects the ancient principle of self-mastery. To adhere to the *Law of Inner Wisdom* is to control the flow of information and emotions within, recognizing that the inner world is just as important as the outer one. Ancient teachings emphasize that wisdom is not simply the accumulation of knowledge but the ability to sift through that knowledge with discernment. Independent thinking ensures that we are not mere followers but individuals capable of determining our own purpose and path in life.

In this context, *The Law of Inner Wisdom* is also about resisting the temptation to speak impulsively. In ancient wisdom traditions, silence and patience are virtues, allowing space for deeper understanding to emerge before speaking or acting. This cultivates the ability to make decisions that reflect wisdom rather than haste, allowing us to contribute meaningfully to both our spiritual and material lives.

Chapter 17: The Law of Positive Speech

To live by the *Law of Positive Speech* is to harness the power of words as a tool for creation, healing, and connection. This principle reminds us that words carry energy and intention, shaping both our inner and outer worlds. Each spoken word is an offering that ripples through the fabric of life, creating waves of positivity or negativity. By choosing to speak with kindness and good intent, we align ourselves with the flow of universal harmony, contributing to the upliftment of all.

To align with the *Law of Positive Speech* and considering the karmic aspect of energy exchange, let's take a look at **Luke 6:45** – *"A good man brings good things out of the good stored up in his heart, and an evil man brings evil things out of the evil stored up in his heart. For the mouth speaks what the heart is full of."* This verse highlights the metaphysical truth that our words are an expression of our inner being. When we speak positively, it reflects the goodness within us and generates positive energy that resonates with the world. The law of compensation plays out as this energy ricochets through the universe, influencing not only the speaker but also everyone impacted by the spoken words.

Metaphysically, words are extensions of our vibrational frequency, and speaking positively of others creates a ripple effect of uplifting energy. When positive words are spoken, they enter the energetic fields of others, causing an uplifting resonance. This energy then ricochets and reverberates, creating a web of interconnected positivity that touches all who come into contact with it. Each positive word amplifies the flow of harmony and balance, generating an expanding network of peace and goodwill.

The energy of kind words returns to the speaker, enriched by the collective response of those who receive them. This energetic exchange is karmic: we receive back the love and positivity that we send into the world, making us participants in a continuous cycle of spiritual growth and upliftment.

Philosophically, the act of speaking positively aligns with the understanding that we are all interconnected. Words are not isolated—they are powerful vibrations that spread through the collective energy field. When positive words are spoken, they bounce back as manifestations of goodwill and trust. This exchange of energy is like a wave: it travels through space and returns magnified, bringing more harmony to all relationships.

In the karmic sense, every word spoken is a seed planted in the cosmic soil. Words of positivity bloom into harmonious relationships, successful endeavors, and a deeper sense of community. By aligning with the *Law of Positive Speech*, we ensure that we contribute to a cycle of uplifting energy that ricochets back to us, bringing blessings, opportunities, and goodwill.

Chapter 18: The Law of Emotional Balance

Emotional stability is a cornerstone of spiritual clarity. To live by the ***Law of Emotional Balance*** is to master the art of navigating life's highs and lows without losing our inner compass. This law reminds us that our emotional world is powerful, but it must be guided by wisdom, not ruled by impulse. While emotions are integral to the human experience, unchecked emotions can lead to chaos, irrational decisions, and spiritual disarray.

Proverbs 14:29 offers this guiding wisdom: *"Whoever is patient has great understanding, but one who is quick-tempered displays folly."* This verse illustrates the importance of patience and emotional regulation. Emotional balance leads to greater wisdom, while being quick-tempered often brings regret and destruction. **James 1:19** further echoes this sentiment: *"Everyone should be quick to listen, slow to speak and slow to become angry."* It reinforces the idea that emotional balance promotes spiritual clarity, preventing unnecessary discord and maintaining harmony in our lives.

Metaphysically, emotions are powerful energy currents that must be channeled with intention and clarity. Emotional imbalance is like a storm that disrupts the harmony within, preventing us from accessing our higher consciousness. Emotions like anger, fear, and envy are of lower vibrations, clouding our judgment and trapping us in reactive cycles. When we stay grounded in emotional balance, we move beyond these reactive states and connect with our higher self.

Remaining balanced with our emotions allows us to ride the waves of life without being overtaken by them. Just as the Earth remains grounded despite the shifting seasons, so too must we remain anchored within ourselves. Emotional balance is not about suppression but about cultivating the ability to *feel* deeply while remaining in control. True emotional mastery lies in our ability to recognize emotions, allow them to pass through, and return to a state of harmony.

Philosophically, maintaining emotional equilibrium reflects our inner wisdom and the cultivation of self-awareness. Emotions can either enlighten or destroy, depending on how we manage them. In ancient philosophy, emotions were viewed as sacred forces, but they required mastery to serve as conduits for higher understanding. In a balanced state, emotions serve to elevate our perception and guide us toward deeper truths. Conversely, when emotions dominate, they can obstruct our path and distort reality.

In ancient wisdom, the ***Law of Compensation*** teaches that what we put out into the universe comes back to us. When our emotions are imbalanced, we create instability in our environment and relationships. Emotional balance, then, becomes a philosophical tool for preserving harmony within and around us. By remaining calm and centered, we cultivate environments of peace and clarity, where wisdom can flourish.

To live by the ***Law of Emotional Balance*** is to recognize the divine responsibility we hold in maintaining our emotional world. By achieving emotional balance, we walk the path of Ma'at, where truth, harmony, and justice prevail, allowing us to navigate life's challenges with a calm and wise heart. We become a reflection of divine order, embodying the strength to maintain our integrity in every emotional storm.

Chapter 19: The Law of Trust

The ***Law of Trust*** speaks to the deeper relationship between humanity and the Divine. Trust, in this sense, is not merely about interpersonal relationships but about placing complete faith in the Creator's wisdom, guidance, and timing. Trust is the acknowledgment that the Divine plan is unfolding perfectly, even when circumstances seem unclear or difficult. It reflects a spiritual surrender, where we allow ourselves to align with the natural order, confident that we are being guided toward our highest good.

Proverbs 3:5-6 tells us, *"Trust in the Lord with all your heart and lean not on your own understanding; in all your ways submit to Him, and He will make your paths straight."* This scripture emphasizes the importance of trusting in the Creator above all, rather than relying solely on our limited perspective. Trust is about having faith in the divine process, knowing that every challenge or success serves a purpose in our spiritual evolution.

Furthermore, Trust is the cornerstone of all meaningful connections, forming the foundation upon which relationships grow and thrive. It is more than an expectation; trust represents a mutual exchange that reflects our integrity and faithfulness. Essential qualities such as dependability, honesty, and consistency reinforce the bonds we share with others, ensuring that trust is earned through steadfast character and honorable behavior, as illustrated in **Proverbs 22:1**, which states, *"A good name is more desirable than great riches; to be esteemed is better than silver or gold."*

Metaphysically, trust serves as the connective tissue between the soul and the Divine. It is through trust that we tap into the higher frequencies of guidance, allowing ourselves to become vessels for divine wisdom and inspiration.

Trust in the Creator means understanding that the universe is working for our growth and that each experience is an opportunity for us to align more deeply with our spiritual purpose.

Philosophically, trust is a declaration of faith that transcends the temporary and the material, connecting us to a reality governed by divine principles. To live by the *Law of Trust* is to walk in confidence, not in our own abilities alone, but in the knowledge that we are supported by a divine order. Trust is the bridge between the seen and the unseen, the known and the unknown, and by trusting in the Creator, we allow ourselves to be guided by a wisdom greater than our own.

The *Law of Trust* reminds us that real trust is rooted in our relationship with the Divine. It is an active, ongoing process of surrender, faith, and alignment with the higher order of the universe. By embracing trust, we open ourselves to divine guidance, secure in the knowledge that we are always supported and led toward our true path.

Chapter 20: The Law of Purity

Purity extends beyond physical cleanliness to encompass the mind, heart, and spirit. ***The Law of Purity*** encourages us to live free from negativity, greed, and dishonesty. **Matthew 5:8** reminds us, *"Blessed are the pure in heart, for they shall see God."* This verse speaks to the spiritual clarity that purity brings, allowing us to connect more deeply with divine presence. Purity paves the way for wisdom, grace, and inner peace, creating a foundation upon which we build a life aligned with the highest truths.

Metaphysically, purity is the channel through which divine energy flows unimpeded. Just as clean water reflects light, a pure heart reflects the divine essence, resonating with clarity and authenticity. Like children, who learn effortlessly and absorb knowledge because they have unclouded minds, purity invites wisdom by removing barriers. A clear mind and spirit create a fertile ground for spiritual growth, where divine insights can take root and flourish.

Purity in thought, surroundings, and body allows divine energy to permeate our being without hindrance, facilitating a deeper connection to universal wisdom. Maintaining purity involves being mindful of our exposure to elements that may taint our physical, mental, and spiritual well-being. This includes educating ourselves about the presence of toxins in food, water, and our environment, as well as identifying low-vibrational influences such as negative relationships and harmful mental attitudes. True purity means recognizing and counterbalancing these sources of contamination with practices that promote simplicity, quietude, and inner clarity. By being intentional about the influences we allow into our lives, we cultivate an environment where our energy remains clear and our minds unclouded.

Philosophically, purity represents the pursuit of a life untainted by ego and superficial desires. It requires continuous dedication to integrity, self-awareness, and resilience in the face of worldly distractions. In striving for purity, we rise above our base instincts, cultivating the virtues that lead to enlightenment. Just as a polished mirror reflects more light, a pure soul reflects the highest principles of wisdom and truth.

The path of purity is not about perfection but about refining our intentions and actions. In ancient wisdom traditions, purity is seen as a way to cleanse the spirit, allowing it to resonate with the harmonious vibrations of the universe. By honoring the *Law of Purity*, we set ourselves on a path of spiritual clarity, where we find strength, wisdom, and an enduring connection to the divine.

To live by the *Law of Purity* is to cultivate a life of clarity, integrity, and spiritual refinement. Purity allows us to maintain a close connection with the divine, ensuring that our hearts, minds, and actions are aligned with the highest truths.

Chapter 21: The Law of Joy

The *Law of Joy* calls us to share a powerful, transformative energy that uplifts and harmonizes the lives of others. This principle reflects a calling to bring light, positivity, and peace into the world. Joy is more than just a temporary feeling; it is a state of being that reflects alignment with divine will and spiritual harmony. By cultivating joy within ourselves and sharing it, we participate in a divine dance of connection, nurturing the world around us.

Proverbs 15:30 – *"Light in a messenger's eyes brings joy to the heart, and good news gives health to the bones."* This verse emphasizes the positive impact of joy and the energy it carries. It suggests that joy is not only beneficial to the soul but also brings health and healing, underscoring the power of spreading happiness and positivity to uplift others.

Metaphysically, joy resonates at a high frequency, influencing the physical and mental states of those who embody it. When we experience joy, endorphins and other positive neurochemicals are released, contributing to improved mental clarity, increased immunity, and overall well-being. Joy is not only beneficial to the body but also to the mind and spirit, as it clears energetic blockages and facilitates a state of flow. *The high vibration of joy attracts abundance, peace, and opportunities* for spiritual growth, forming a powerful catalyst for personal transformation.

Philosophically, joy is a profound expression of the soul's freedom and resilience. It reflects an ability to rise above life's challenges and connect to something greater than oneself. Ancient wisdom teaches that joy is linked to virtues such as gratitude, compassion, and humility, guiding one to live with a sense of purpose and reverence. True joy is not contingent upon external circumstances; it emerges from a deep alignment with righteousness and truth, enabling one to face adversity with grace and positivity. In this way, spreading joy becomes an act of service, helping others to see life's beauty and potential, no matter their circumstances.

To embody the *Law of Joy* is to carry light into the world, creating a space of positivity and healing. Joy is a contagious force that, when shared, elevates not only the individual but also those around them. By living joyfully, we align ourselves with divine truth, contributing to a world infused with love, laughter, and an abiding sense of peace.

Chapter 22: The Law of Effort

The ***Law of Effort*** calls us to engage with life wholeheartedly, putting forth our fullest effort and highest intention. This principle encourages us to live authentically and purposefully, aiming to make a positive impact on the world around us. By striving for excellence, we invite the divine to support our efforts, transforming our actions into expressions of our highest self.

Colossians 3:23 – *"Whatever you do, work at it with all your heart, as working for the Lord, not for human masters."* This verse reminds us that our best efforts are not just for personal gain but for the fulfillment of a higher purpose. When we commit ourselves fully to our tasks with sincere intention, we align with divine support and bring value to all that we do.

Metaphysically, living by the ***Law of Effort*** is an act of co-creation with the universe. Our intentions, when aligned with our actions, create powerful energy that reverberates outward, drawing opportunities and support from the divine. The energy of authentic effort elevates our consciousness and attracts resources that enhance our path. When we engage fully, we are participating in a sacred dance with the cosmos, activating potential within ourselves and harmonizing with the world around us. In this way, each step we take in giving our best allows us to shape the reality we desire.

Philosophically, the commitment to doing our best reflects an adherence to the law of compensation. When we give our best, we set into motion a cycle of cause and effect, which naturally brings forth positive outcomes. In ancient wisdom, the pursuit of excellence is seen as a reflection of one's inner character. It is the path of the seeker who understands that every action carries meaning and that true fulfillment is achieved not by shortcuts, but by dedication, patience, and effort. By living in alignment with our highest ideals, we contribute to the collective good, knowing that the energy we invest in our work ultimately returns to us manifold.

To live by the ***Law of Effort*** is to honor the sacred potential within us, acting as vessels of divine will. When we commit ourselves fully, with an unwavering heart and spirit, we create ripples of positivity that influence both ourselves and the world around us. In this way, we contribute to the unfolding of a reality rooted in truth, integrity, and divine purpose, allowing us to shine as reflections of the Creator's wisdom.

Chapter 23: The Law of Compassionate Communication

The ***Law of Compassionate Communication*** reflects the importance of empathy, understanding, and positive intent in all our interactions. Just as a mother speaks with gentleness to her child, compassionate communication involves actively listening and speaking with love, aiming to uplift, heal, and develop connection. True compassion in communication is about engaging with others in a way that recognizes and honors their unique perspectives and experiences.

Ephesians 4:29 – *"Let no corrupting talk come out of your mouths, but only such as is good for building up, as fits the occasion, that it may give grace to those who hear."* This verse highlights the value of compassionate and constructive speech, emphasizing that our words should bring kindness, healing, and encouragement to others. When we communicate with compassion, we create an environment where positive energy and mutual respect flourish.

Metaphysically, compassionate communication is an energy exchange that extends beyond the spoken word. Words carry vibrations, and when spoken with compassion, they emit a frequency that harmonizes with the divine order. Just as ripples form when a stone is dropped into water, compassionate words create waves of positive energy that affect both the speaker and the listener. Communication rooted in compassion has the potential to uplift, inspire, and bring peace, as it aligns our intentions with the highest frequencies of love and empathy.

Philosophically, compassionate communication is an expression of our interconnectedness. Speaking with kindness and empathy is an acknowledgment of the shared human experience, promoting unity and understanding. In ancient wisdom traditions, words were seen as manifestations of spirit and energy. By choosing to speak compassionately, we align with the virtues of patience, humility, and respect. Communication becomes a tool for healing, reinforcing the law of reciprocity: the more love and understanding we offer, the more we receive in return. This virtuous cycle deepens our connections with others and enriches our own lives, aligning us with the natural order of balance and mutual respect.

To honor the ***Law of Compassionate Communication*** is to embrace the transformative power of words as vehicles of love and understanding. By speaking with positive intent, we become conduits of healing energy, capable of reaching hearts and bridging divides. In every conversation, we have the opportunity to bring light, joy, and peace into the lives of those we encounter, creating a ripple effect that ultimately contributes to a more harmonious and compassionate world.

Chapter 24: The Law of Opposing Opinions

The ***Law of Opposing Opinions*** underscores the importance of embracing diverse perspectives. In our journey of growth and self-improvement, listening to views that challenge our own expands our understanding, cultivates humility, and refines our thoughts. This practice not only broadens our knowledge but also strengthens our ability to engage in meaningful discourse and find common ground. Listening to opposing opinions helps check the ego, ensuring we aren't high-minded and that we remain vigilant to the potential blind spots in our thinking.

Proverbs 15:31 – *"Whoever heeds life-giving correction will be at home among the wise."* This verse highlights the value of listening to feedback, even when it may challenge our current beliefs. By welcoming differing perspectives, we cultivate wisdom and allow ourselves to be enriched by the viewpoints of others, enhancing our journey toward personal growth and understanding.

Metaphysically, listening to opposing opinions is an exercise in expanding consciousness. By engaging with perspectives that differ from our own, we challenge the boundaries of our understanding and allow for the integration of new insights. This practice helps dissolve the ego, which often limits us to a single perspective, and aligns us with the flow of universal wisdom. By remaining open, we can uncover deeper truths that reside within the diversity of thought, recognizing that each perspective contributes a unique piece to the broader mosaic of knowledge.

Philosophically, the ***Law of Opposing Opinions*** reflects the virtues of humility, patience, and intellectual curiosity. Ancient teachings highlight the importance of a balanced mind, one that seeks understanding from all angles. In honoring this principle, we step beyond personal biases, acknowledging that the collective wisdom of humanity arises from a multitude of voices. Much like the roundtable, where all viewpoints are welcome, we open the floor to diverse perspectives that refine and elevate the conversation. This approach develops a spirit of collaboration, leading to a more profound comprehension of truth.

To live by the ***Law of Opposing Opinions*** is to embrace a life of continual learning, humility, and connection. When we open ourselves to perspectives that challenge our own, we not only expand our understanding but also contribute to a more inclusive, compassionate, and harmonious world. This practice reflects a commitment to growth and a willingness to expand beyond the limitations of individual perspective, embracing the vastness of collective wisdom.

Chapter 25: The Law of Harmony

The *Law of Harmony* emphasizes our responsibility to cultivate spaces of peace, understanding, and positive energy. According to Hermetic teachings, harmony reflects the balanced interaction of dual aspects within ourselves and the universe. This law encourages us to be intentional in raising the vibrational frequency around us, creating environments where growth, love, and unity can thrive. In our personal, communal, and universal spaces, harmony is essential for aligning with the natural order, which in turn promotes spiritual enlightenment. As we embody harmony, we emanate high-vibrational energy, enhancing every space we inhabit and contributing to the interconnected flow of the universe.

Hebrews 12:14 – *"Make every effort to live in peace with everyone and to be holy; without holiness, no one will see the Lord."* This verse highlights the active pursuit of peace and harmony as a form of sacred duty. It reinforces the idea that harmony is not just a personal endeavor but a divine obligation, essential for spiritual alignment and growth.

Metaphysically, harmony is the original and natural state of the universe, where all things exist in a state of balance. As beings in tune with divine energy, we have the power to affect the spaces we inhabit. When we create harmony, we channel the divine order that flows through us into the world around us, restoring and enhancing the vibrational energy of our environment. This active alignment allows us to become co-creators in the universe's ongoing expression of beauty and balance. Each act of harmony uplifts not only ourselves but also those in our energetic grids, generating spiritual growth and positive transformation.

Philosophically, this perspective is rooted in ancient wisdom, creating harmony is both a virtue and a duty. It is a manifestation of our commitment to live in alignment with higher principles. The ancients believed that harmony reflected divine justice, where everything was in its rightful place, maintaining equilibrium. In this context, our actions, words, and thoughts should aim to bring harmony, as this reflects a life of virtue and purpose. Through patience, kindness, and an awareness of interconnectedness, we can facilitate balance in our surroundings, nurturing a collective sense of well-being and unity. Like a skilled musician contributing to a symphony, we harmonize with people, places and things, blending our individual energies much like how a composer carefully selects notes, tones, and rhythms to create melodies. Each person, like an instrument in an orchestra, contributes unique frequencies that, when combined, bring forth a profound beauty that resonates through all of existence.

To embody the *Law of Harmony* is to be a conscious architect of peace and balance. As divine beings, it is our sacred duty to elevate and harmonize the spaces we inhabit, recognizing that each of our actions reverberates across the fabric of life.

Chapter 26: The Law of Laughter

Invoking laughter is akin to the work of a spiritual alchemist, seeking to discover the hidden recipes for joy and happiness and sharing them with the world. In the *Law of Laughter,* we recognize that laughter is not merely a response to humor but a powerful energy that uplifts, heals, and connects. Just as an alchemist seeks the essence of transformation, we too become creators of joyful energy, stirring laughter in others to bring lightness and healing to the world.

Ecclesiastes 3:4 — *"A time to weep, and a time to laugh; a time to mourn, and a time to dance."* This verse reminds us of the natural cycles of life and the balance between joy and sorrow. It reinforces the idea that laughter, like all things, has its place and time, and when invoked, it brings harmony, release, and renewal to the soul.

Metaphysically, laughter is one of the highest frequencies of energy, capable of shifting the vibrations within and around us. Like an alchemical catalyst, laughter activates a joyful state that spreads and elevates the collective mood, promoting health and resilience. It purifies the spirit, transforming stagnant energy and creating a flow of positivity. By invoking laughter, we clear out emotional blockages and align ourselves with the lightness of the soul, enabling us to engage with life's challenges from a place of ease and grace. Laughter is truly a gift, allowing us to experience a direct connection to the divine joy that permeates the universe.

Philosophically, laughter symbolizes resilience, embodying the wisdom to embrace lightness in the face of adversity. The ancient sages recognized the power of joy as a reflection of an enlightened soul. They understood that laughter is a response not only to the humorous but also to the absurdities and paradoxes of existence. Through laughter, we find unity in shared human experience, affirming the beauty of imperfection and the acceptance of life as it is. Like the alchemist's golden elixir, laughter is a transformative force that strengthens our spirit, builds community, and reminds us that joy is an integral part of the human journey.

To live by the ***Law of Laughter*** is to bring the energy of joy and lightness wherever we go. We become agents of positive change, much like spiritual comedians who, through compassion and insight, bring healing to others. Laughter goes beyond language and cultural barriers, creating an atmosphere of love, peace, and connection. By embracing the alchemical power of laughter, we contribute to a world where joy is abundant, and our collective spirit is uplifted.

Chapter 27: The Law of Openness to Love

To live by the ***Law of Openness to Love*** is to recognize that love is not a one-dimensional force; it is multifaceted, flowing through creation in ways that reflect the infinite nature of the Creator. Love can be found in friendship, acts of kindness, nature's beauty, the multitude of creatures in the environment, and the support of family and community. This principle calls us to attune ourselves to the subtle ways in which divine love expresses itself, not merely in romantic or idealized visions of love but in the everyday connections that enrich our lives.

1 John 4:16 – *"And so we know and rely on the love God has for us. God is love. Whoever lives in love lives in God, and God in them."* This verse reminds us that love, in all its expressions, is a reflection of the divine essence. When we are open to love, we embrace a deeper connection with the Creator, experiencing the divine presence in the many forms love takes in our lives.

Metaphysically, love is the highest frequency, a sacred energy that aligns us with the Creator's will. On a deeper level, love is not merely an emotion but the fundamental force that binds the universe together. The Bible tells us that *"God is love,"* and metaphysically, this suggests that love is the creative essence of all existence—a universal "glue" that upholds the structure and harmony of creation. Love also exemplifies the **Law of Attraction**, as it resonates with the pure, divine frequency that draws all things toward wholeness.

Just as sunlight can be refracted into a spectrum of colors, divine love expresses itself in diverse ways, each a unique form of divine intelligence. When we remain open to love, we allow these energies to nourish our soul and elevate our spirit, strengthening our connection to the source of all creation. Love invites us to trust that the Creator provides what we need, even in forms we may not initially recognize.

Philosophically, the *Law of Openness to Love* requires discernment, humility, and awareness. Love should not be mistaken for mere sentimentality; rather, it is the foundation of meaningful connections and the force that binds us to others in a network of compassion and respect. Ancient wisdom teaches us that true love, whether it be in friendships, family bonds, or our interactions with the natural world, calls us to see beyond ourselves. By embracing diverse forms of love, we cultivate a fuller experience of life, one that reflects the richness of creation. Just as a skilled alchemist discerns between materials to create a balanced potion, we are called to recognize the forms of love that bring growth and harmony, avoiding false loves that distort or drain our energy.

Welcoming love in its many forms allows us to embrace the Creator's boundless ways of connecting with us. In doing so, we honor the divine, inviting its presence to uplift our relationships, deepen our understanding, and illuminate our path. Being open to love is not about indiscriminately accepting all things, but rather about recognizing the divine spark within each connection, allowing it to transform and uplift us in alignment with our highest truth.

Chapter 28: The Law of Forgiveness

The ***Law of Forgiveness*** teaches us to release ourselves from the chains of resentment, recognizing that holding onto anger or pain can harm the soul. This principle reminds us that forgiveness is as much for the person forgiving as it is for the one being forgiven. When we forgive, we let go of toxic energy, allowing our spirits to heal and grow. We come to understand that forgiveness is a path to peace and a practice of compassion.

Mark 11:25 – *"And when you stand praying, if you hold anything against anyone, forgive them, so that your Father in heaven may forgive you your sins."* This verse underscores the reciprocal nature of forgiveness; by releasing others, we too are released. It highlights forgiveness as an act of grace, opening the door to divine mercy and healing.

Metaphysically, forgiveness is a process of clearing blocked energy, releasing emotions like anger, hatred, or resentment that, if left unchecked, can manifest on the physical plan as bodily or mental ailments. When we forgive, we transmute negative energies and allow positive, healing vibrations to fill the space, creating a profound sense of inner peace. Forgiveness allows us to align with the universal flow, inviting light and love to replace darkness. Through forgiveness, we elevate our consciousness, moving beyond the lower vibrations of blame and guilt to reach a state of spiritual equilibrium.

Philosophically, forgiveness embodies the virtues of humility, wisdom, and empathy. In the teachings of ancient wisdom, forgiveness is seen as an expression of inner strength and an understanding that no one is perfect. To forgive others for their mistakes is to acknowledge our shared human frailty. When we forgive, we reflect divine mercy, realizing that forgiveness is a choice to release judgment and embrace compassion. Ancient philosophies often encourage us to "guard the heart," suggesting that the act of forgiveness shields the heart from bitterness and preserves our integrity.

To live by the ***Law of Forgiveness*** is to let go of burdens that keep us from experiencing joy and peace. Forgiveness is an invitation to move forward with clarity, without the shadows of resentment clouding our journey. By embracing forgiveness, we release ourselves from the prison of past hurts, allowing our spirits to be free and our hearts to remain open to love and divine connection.

Chapter 29: The Law of Kindness

The ***Law of Kindness*** is an intentional choice to radiate goodness, embodying the light and love we wish to see in the world. This principle is not merely about indiscriminate niceness but about reflecting the divine qualities of love, compassion, and understanding in every action. Kindness goes beyond passive goodwill; it is an active force that shapes our reality in a harmonious way, uplifting our interactions and creating a ripple effect of positivity that impacts the lives of those around us.

When we express kindness, we draw out the divine will within creation, allowing the God within all things to shine. Since God is love, each act of kindness inspires a greater expression of love in the world, inviting the divine essence to manifest in and through us.

Galatians 6:10 – *"So then, whenever we have an opportunity, let us work for the good of all, and especially for those Of the family of faith."* This verse underscores the principle of kindness as an act of responsibility, one that should be extended not only to those closest to us but to all humanity. By choosing to embody kindness, we reflect the goodness of divine love in our actions.

Metaphysically, kindness is an energetic expression that resonates with the law of attraction. Acts of kindness elevate the vibrations of both the giver and the receiver, creating a cycle of positive energy. When we radiate kindness, we align ourselves with the highest frequencies of love and compassion. This vibrational alignment attracts similar energy, enriching our lives and creating harmonious relationships. Kindness also enhances our spiritual path by opening us to deeper levels of connection, empathy, and understanding. In essence, kindness aligns us with the universal law of cause and effect, allowing us to send out love and positivity, which inevitably returns to us in abundant forms.

Philosophically, kindness can be seen as a virtue that expresses our interconnectedness with all beings. Ancient teachings suggest that kindness is a reflection of the divine within us and a recognition of the divine in others. This virtue is about treating others with respect and dignity, recognizing that every interaction is an opportunity to uplift, support, and contribute positively to the lives of others. Through kindness, we take on the role of co-creators, shaping our world with love and integrity. Just as a plant grows stronger with nurturing care, so too do relationships and communities thrive in an environment of kindness.

Embodying the *Law of Kindness* brings light, warmth, and healing into the world. Kindness creates a ripple effect, extending far beyond the initial act, touching lives in ways we may never see. By embracing kindness, we align ourselves with the divine, becoming channels of love, compassion, and positive change. As we practice kindness, we find that it transforms both the giver and the receiver, enriching our lives with a profound sense of purpose and fulfillment.

Chapter 30: The Law of Considerate Conduct

The **Law of Considerate Conduct** calls us to engage with others from our highest, most authentic selves, embodying qualities of respect, awareness, strength, and godliness. Acting respectfully toward others in all areas of life—whether with family, friends, business partners, or loved ones—promotes harmony and cooperation. By observing this law, we cultivate an environment of mutual trust, helping to preserve the balance and integrity of our personal and communal lives. Respectful conduct is more than courtesy; it is a commitment to honoring the dignity of others, thus promoting a harmonious atmosphere that benefits all.

1 Peter 2:17 advises, *"Show proper respect to everyone, love the family of believers, fear God, honor the emperor."* This verse emphasizes that respect is not confined to specific relationships but extends to all individuals, promoting harmony and mutual regard. Similarly, in **Philippians 2:3**, we are reminded, *"Do nothing out of selfish ambition or vain conceit. Rather, in humility value others above yourselves."* These teachings highlight the value of humility and respect, underscoring the law's essence in promoting peace and honoring others in our actions.

Metaphysically, acting respectfully stems from a deep alignment with our authentic self, which inherently embodies qualities of Ma'at, such as harmony, balance, and truth. When we honor the **Law of Considerate Conduct**, we become representatives of this divine principle, embodying qualities that promote cooperative and harmonious relations. In each interaction, we choose to operate from a place of authenticity, integrity, and alignment with universal laws. This approach to life allows us to uphold harmony and encourages mutual respect, bringing us closer to our true purpose and strengthening our connection with the divine.

Philosophically, the *Law of Considerate Conduct* reflects the importance of maintaining balance in relationships and communities. When we act with consideration, we avoid actions that might transgress or trespass against others, which could lead to imbalance and even war. This balance is essential for preventing disruptions in personal and professional realms, promoting peace, and averting conflicts or misunderstandings. By adhering to this principle, we contribute to a stable environment that supports growth, cooperation, and collective well-being.

Living by the *Law of Considerate Conduct* is a commitment to honoring others and creating harmonious connections. This principle reminds us that each respectful act strengthens the bonds within our community, cultivating a supportive environment where all can thrive. By conducting ourselves with kindness, consideration, and integrity, we align with divine principles, promoting harmony and inspiring others to do the same. This law encourages us to walk in alignment with our higher purpose, honoring the sacred connection we share with others and reinforcing the collective balance essential to a life of peace and fulfillment.

Chapter 31: The Law of Acceptance

The **_Law of Acceptance_** teaches us to approach life and others without egoistic discrimination. Acceptance does not mean tolerating injustice or negativity; rather, it involves the humility to recognize that each person, event, or circumstance appears at a specific stage of development. When we accept people where they are, without judgment or expectation, we cultivate a deeper understanding and respect for the diversity of life's paths. The more we are able to observe the diversity of life, the more we are able to contribute to that diversity in meaningful ways.

Romans 15:7 offers insight into this principle: _"Accept one another, then, just as Christ accepted you, in order to bring praise to God."_ This verse speaks to the importance of embracing others as they are, without imposing conditions or judgments. In doing so, we reflect a divine love that surpasses superficial differences, allowing us to uplift one another and honor the divine within each person.

Metaphysically, acceptance aligns us with the flow of divine energy, allowing us to observe life with an open heart. True acceptance requires the intelligence to discern when it is appropriate to embrace the present moment without attachment or resistance. By acknowledging the unique circumstances that arise on each path, we learn to let go of control, trusting that the universe is always guiding us toward growth and self-realization. Acceptance becomes a practice of releasing expectations, which liberates us from the frustrations of unmet desires and keeps us open to the lessons that each experience brings.

Philosophically, acceptance reflects the virtues of patience, compassion, and wisdom. In ancient wisdom, acceptance was understood as a quality of the enlightened mind—one that observes without reacting, that understands without imposing. By being receptive to the unique stages of life's manifestations, we cultivate a peaceful heart, free from the tension and division created by judgment. Acceptance is not passive but is instead an active choice to meet the world with kindness and understanding. This approach opens us to a reality where diverse perspectives are valued and where growth is facilitated by honoring the individuality of each journey.

To live by the *Law of Acceptance* is to move through life with grace, seeing the divine potential in all things. Through acceptance, we build a foundation of inner peace, allowing us to experience a greater sense of unity with the world around us. We open ourselves to life's full spectrum, understanding that every moment is part of a greater cosmic order, inviting us to grow, learn, and contribute to the harmony of existence.

Chapter 32: The Law of Inner Guidance

Following inner guidance is a profound spiritual principle that speaks to the heart of intuition, divine connection, and spiritual maturity. The ***Law of Inner Guidance*** emphasizes the significance of tuning into our inner voice, which serves as a bridge between us and the Creator. This law reflects the highest form of self-trust and aligns us with divine will, allowing us to navigate life with clarity, accuracy, and purpose.

Proverbs 20:27 beautifully states, *"The human spirit is the lamp of the Lord that sheds light on one's inmost being."* This verse conveys the deep spiritual truth that our inner guidance is not separate from the divine but a direct expression of it. Through our inner voice, we receive illumination and insight from the Creator, guiding us toward decisions and paths that align with divine purpose.

Isaiah 30:21 supports this concept: *"Whether you turn to the right or to the left, your ears will hear a voice behind you, saying, 'This is the way; walk in it.'"* This verse illustrates the constant presence of divine guidance available to us, reinforcing the idea that by listening to our inner wisdom, we can confidently move through life.

Metaphysically, inner guidance is an aspect of our intuitive nature, the voice of the spirit that enables us to tap into the universal or cosmic mind. This guidance is an internal compass that reflects our ability to connect with the divine consciousness, bringing clarity and insight beyond intellectual understanding. By listening to this voice, we align ourselves with a flow of wisdom that extends beyond individual thought and connects us with the broader currents of the universe.

The process of developing this inner guidance requires cultivating inner stillness and trust in the divine order. As we refine our ability to listen to our inner voice, we learn to discern the difference between fear-based reactions and true intuitive insights. This cultivation brings about a higher degree of spiritual discernment and allows us to align our actions and decisions with our soul's journey. As we grow spiritually, our inner guidance becomes an indispensable tool for navigating the complexities of life, leading us towards paths of wisdom, growth, and purpose.

Philosophically, this perspective is rooted in ancient wisdom, following inner guidance is about personal responsibility and spiritual integrity. This practice reflects the ability to trust in the wisdom that emerges from within, emphasizing the importance of listening to one's internal perspective as a reliable source of guidance. It speaks to the principle of self-reliance, where one draws wisdom not from external validation but from an inner reservoir of knowledge, intuition, and spiritual alignment. By developing an inner trust in our internal perspective, we deepen our connection to truth and strengthen our ability to make choices that align with our highest purpose. Inner guidance thus becomes the compass by which we navigate the moral and spiritual complexities of life, aligning ourselves with higher laws and principles. The ability to follow one's intuition and inner compass was seen as essential for maintaining balance with the divine order.

To live by the ***Law of Inner Guidance*** is to trust in the divine connection that flows through us, embracing intuition as a guiding force for wisdom and aligning with our highest truth. This law encourages self-sufficiency, as we cultivate the higher faculties of our mind—enhancing knowledge, intuition, and the ability to be guided by our inner voice, which reflects the wisdom of the higher self. By tuning into our inner guidance, we navigate life with a sense of purpose, confidence, and alignment with the Creator. This practice requires faith, inner stillness, and spiritual maturity as we continually learn to listen and respond to the inner voice that directs us on the path of righteousness and spiritual fulfillment.

Chapter 33: The Law of Conversing with Awareness

The ***Law of Conversing with Awareness*** emphasizes the transformative power of mindful communication as a tool for spiritual growth and self-discovery. **Proverbs 15:28** offers, *"The heart of the righteous weighs its answers, but the mouth of the wicked gushes evil."* This verse underscores the importance of thoughtful speech, encouraging us to approach conversations with a sense of awareness and intention, mindful of the energy and influence our words carry. When we communicate, we must be fully present, considering the trajectory and the cause-and-effect of our words as they ripple outward, impacting both ourselves and others. Communication is not limited to spoken words; it can also be expressed through meditation, as we connect with God, the universe, and the energies around us. In these moments of silent communication, the same awareness is required to align ourselves with higher truth and intention. **Proverbs 16:24** further illuminates this law: *"Gracious words are a honeycomb, sweet to the soul and healing to the bones."* This verse reveals how kind and mindful words bring healing and harmony, reinforcing the positive effects of conversing with awareness in every interaction.

Metaphysically, conversing with awareness represents an alignment with higher knowledge and the universal principles that govern existence. When we engage in conversation from the perspective of mindful awareness, we are not merely exchanging words; we are channeling reflections of our higher self, sharing insights distilled from inner contemplation. Speaking with full awareness means that we communicate from a grand perspective, one that is informed by the cosmic laws. These laws include *Mentalism*, which asserts that the universe is a product of the mind; *Correspondence*, which highlights the connection between all levels of existence; *Vibration*, which teaches that everything is in constant motion;

Polarity, which illustrates the dual nature of reality; *Rhythm*, which shows that all things have natural cycles; *Cause and Effect*, which emphasizes the interconnectivity of all actions; and *Gender*, which represents balance and creative forces. With this understanding, our words become vessels of truth, carrying forward the essence of our spiritual awareness and alignment with these principles.

Philosophically, this perspective is rooted in ancient wisdom, conversing with awareness reflects the concept of mindful presence and respect for the sacred exchange of ideas. Words are not to be taken lightly; they carry the weight of intention and the power to create, transform, and influence. In conversations, we position ourselves as both students and teachers, engaging with the wisdom inherent in every interaction. By being present and attentive, we honor the unique perspectives of others and create a dynamic space for growth, empathy, and connection. This approach embodies the timeless principles of balance, unity, and harmony, reinforcing our interconnectedness and shared journey on the path of enlightenment. Each conversation, when conducted with awareness, reminds us of the profound truths that shape both our internal and external realities.

To live by the ***Law of Conversing*** with Awareness is to embrace each conversation as an opportunity for spiritual alignment and mutual upliftment. Through mindful communication, we deepen our awareness, further our understanding, and create a harmonious exchange of ideas. In doing so, we align with the divine purpose of words, using them as tools to inspire, heal, and illuminate the path for ourselves and others.

Chapter 34: The Law of Goodness

The ***Law of Goodness*** underscores our responsibility as divine beings to act in ways that uplift and benefit the world around us. In this dualistic environment, there are those who operate in the shadows, and there are those who walk in the light. As sovereign creations of the One Creator, our purpose is to embody goodness, reflecting the divine order through our actions. **Galatians 6:9** reminds us, *"Let us not grow weary in doing good, for at the proper time we will reap a harvest if we do not give up."* This verse speaks to the enduring nature of goodness, encouraging perseverance in righteous deeds and promising a spiritual reward for those who remain steadfast in their commitment to positive action.

Metaphysically, doing good resonates with the principles of universal reciprocity and cosmic harmony. Every act of goodness is a manifestation of divine energy that ripples throughout the fabric of creation. By consciously choosing to perform kind acts, we align ourselves with the flow of positive energy that sustains the universe. The law of reciprocity teaches us that the energy we put forth returns to us, magnified. Good deeds are, therefore, not isolated acts but threads woven into the larger "fabric" of existence, reflecting the interconnected nature of all things. Each act of goodness amplifies our alignment with universal order, contributing to our spiritual evolution and creating a cycle of blessings that perpetuates harmony within and around us.

Philosophically, doing good reflects a deep understanding of the values of kindness, compassion, and justice. Ancient teachings remind us that goodness is a duty of the enlightened, who recognize their roles as stewards of life and creation. A life dedicated to doing good demonstrates an active commitment to justice, mercy, and compassion. In the context of ancient wisdom, good deeds are understood not as isolated actions but as expressions of an enlightened state of being, where one seeks to uplift others and advance the common good. When we act in alignment with goodness, we honor our shared humanity and reinforce our connection to the divine. This perspective echoes the principle that those who embody virtue reflect the qualities of the Creator, thus influencing the world in transformative ways.

To embrace the **_Law of Goodness_** is to recognize the profound impact of our actions. Doing good is not simply an act of generosity but an embodiment of divine love, an acknowledgment of our sacred duty to uplift others, and a manifestation of the divine order within us. By choosing to do good, we contribute to a cycle of positive energy that resonates through all dimensions of existence, supporting the spiritual growth of ourselves and the world around us.

Chapter 35: The Law of Blessings

The *Law of Blessings* reminds us of our role as vessels through which divine energy flows. Just as the Creator is both a source and giver of blessings, we are called to emulate this example, radiating blessings to uplift those around us. When we embody and share blessings, we act as channels of divine grace, bringing love, compassion, and positive energy into the world. **Luke 6:38** reflects this concept: *"Give, and it will be given to you. A good measure, pressed down, shaken together and running over, will be poured into your lap. For with the measure you use, it will be measured to you."* This verse reinforces the reciprocity of blessings—by giving freely, we open ourselves to receiving in even greater abundance.

Metaphysically, giving blessings allows us to tap into a continuous flow of divine energy. Each time we bless others, we not only uplift their spirits but also amplify our own energy field, receiving replenishment from the Creator. Just as a well overflows when it is full, our capacity to give is directly replenished by the divine source, reinforcing that blessings are an infinite resource. The act of blessing others helps to align us with the vibrational energy of love and abundance, creating a ripple effect that expands through the collective consciousness. By blessing, we engage in an exchange of divine energy, ensuring that as we pour out, we are simultaneously refilled, reinforcing the interconnectedness of all life.

Philosophically, giving blessings is rooted in gratitude and selflessness. Ancient wisdom teaches that when we recognize the abundance within our own lives, we naturally desire to share it with others. This act is not simply an expression of generosity but a deep acknowledgment of the universal truth that the more we give, the more we receive. Blessings, in this light, are not bound by material wealth but are spiritual exchanges that carry profound power. By giving blessings, we are contributing to the collective well-being, reinforcing a life of interconnectedness where each individual's actions uplift the whole. This reciprocal nature of blessings creates a framework for communal harmony, ensuring that generosity is met with gratitude, and kindness is met with kindness.

To live by the ***Law of Blessings*** is to act as a radiant source of positivity and grace. Through our words, actions, and presence, we have the ability to transmit divine energy, sharing light with others. By embracing this role, we align ourselves with the abundant flow of the universe, and in doing so, we elevate not only ourselves but all those we encounter. In blessing others, we actively participate in the cosmic cycle of giving and receiving, embodying the divine essence that connects and sustains all of creation.

Chapter 36: The Law of Pure Waters

The ***Law of Pure Waters*** emphasizes the sacred nature of water, not only as a physical substance but as a profound symbol of clarity, memory, and spiritual alignment. Water holds a significant place in both the human body and the planet, acting as a vessel for memory and a medium for life's energy. This law calls us to maintain purity in our internal waters, such as the cerebrospinal fluid that supports our central nervous system, as well as the external waters that sustain the world around us. Just as we strive to keep our thoughts, emotions, and spiritual essence untainted, we are also entrusted with the care of Earth's waters. **John 4:14** offers insight into the power of water as a metaphor for life and purity: *"Whoever drinks the water I give them will never thirst. Indeed, the water I give them will become in them a spring of water welling up to eternal life."* This verse reflects the idea that pure, life-giving waters are a pathway to spiritual abundance, underscoring our responsibility to honor and preserve both the waters within us and around us.

Metaphysically, water is a profound symbol of life, memory, and the flow of divine energy. The purity of water reflects the clarity of our thoughts and the openness of our spiritual connection. Just as water holds the memory of its interactions, our internal "waters" carry the imprints of our thoughts, emotions, and spiritual practices. Isn't it remarkable that these internal waters connect with our "e-motions"—energies in motion, much like the waves on a vast ocean? Emotions move within us like the tides, shaping our inner world with their currents. To keep the waters pure is to maintain a state of mental and emotional clarity, ensuring that our thoughts and actions align with our highest spiritual ideals. In this way, water becomes a reflection of our inner landscape—clear, pure waters allow for an unhindered flow of divine wisdom, enhancing our spiritual journey and grounding us deeply in our purpose.

Philosophically, maintaining the purity of water aligns with the flow and rhythm that sustain all life. In ancient wisdom, water represents not only the physical nourishment of life but also the fluidity, adaptability, and vibrational resonance essential to spiritual harmony. When water is pure, its vibrations are heightened, amplifying its harmony with universal rhythms. By keeping the waters pure, we align ourselves with these higher frequencies, honoring the natural synchronicity that governs all creation. This principle calls us to recognize that purity—whether in thought, action, or environment—supports a harmonious flow within the universe. Just as water moves and adapts, maintaining its clarity and rhythm, so must we respect and preserve the purity around us, understanding that the vitality of life itself is sustained through this interconnected flow.

To uphold the *Law of Pure Waters* is to take responsibility for the physical and spiritual waters that sustain us. Water is synonymous with rhythm, embodying the natural flow and vibration that permeate all existence. We live immersed in water, from the air we breathe, filled with water vapor, to the waters above, below, and around us. Every cell in our body is bathed in water, and even our words carry water vapor as we speak. This pervasive presence of water is a reminder of our interconnectedness with its rhythm and purity. Through this practice, we purify our inner being, ensuring that our thoughts, emotions, and intentions resonate harmoniously with divine order. By maintaining this purity, we act as custodians of life, safeguarding the essence of creation and contributing to a world where the waters remain clear, life-giving, and aligned with the natural flow of the universe.

Chapter 37: The Law of Speaking with Good Intent

The *Law of Speaking with Good Intent*, in alignment with the principles of Ma'at, calls us to communicate with profound intention, aligning our words with our higher nature and divine purpose. This principle is not merely about avoiding negativity but about embracing our role as messengers of divine insight. We are encouraged to speak from a place of elevated consciousness, conveying thoughts born from deep meditation, spiritual revelations, and careful discernment. Our words should reflect the wisdom and guidance we gain through life's experiences, personal growth, and conscious awareness, resonating with the essence of truth and virtue.

James 3:17 captures this beautifully: *"But the wisdom that comes from heaven is first of all pure; then peace-loving, considerate, submissive, full of mercy and good fruit, impartial and sincere."* This verse reminds us that when we speak from a place of good intent, rooted in divine understanding, our words have the power to inspire, uplift, and harmonize, acting as expressions of the higher self in alignment with Ma'at's order.

Metaphysically, words are carriers of vibration, influencing not only our immediate environment but resonating through the energetic fields we inhabit. When we speak with good intent, we align with high frequencies that uplift, promote peace, and encourage balance. It is about speaking from the vantage point of good intentions, embodying the qualities of a person of integrity who channels divine energy. Our words, infused with this positive energy, ripple outward like light penetrating the darkness, shaping the reality we share. By consciously choosing to speak with awareness and mindfulness, we actively contribute to a world that reflects love, truth, and compassion, allowing our words to manifest a harmonious reality that nurtures and uplifts.

Philosophically, speaking with good intent reflects our dedication to personal integrity and self-awareness. To engage in this practice is to embody a life of virtue and to honor the divine in every word. Speaking from a place of good intent requires a mindful commitment to deliver words that resonate with honesty, humility, and respect. By consciously refraining from unintentional or negative conversations and engaging in uplifting discourse, we align ourselves with the ancient principles that saw language as sacred. In choosing our words mindfully, we honor not only the dignity of others but also the cosmic laws that guide harmonious existence. Good intent becomes a guiding principle, promoting respect, empathy, and deeper understanding in all our interactions.

When we speak with good intent, it prompts us to reflect, analyze, and think deeply about our words, connecting us to both our heart and our higher mind. This mindful approach amplifies our vibrational resonance, allowing our words to carry greater impact. Through this process, our speech becomes a powerful force that touches others, creating an energy that uplifts and aligns with the universal flow.

To embody the *Law of Speaking with Good Intent* is not only to be mindful of the impact our words have on others but also to recognize the driving force of intention behind each utterance. Speaking with good intent means allowing our words to flow from a place of honor, integrity, and virtue, shaping them with the purpose of healing, uplifting, and inspiring. When we understand the energy carried by our intentions, our words become powerful vibrations that can resonate deeply with others. This awareness reaches beyond language itself, aligning us with the essence of goodness and positive influence that the law seeks to cultivate.

Chapter 38: The Law of Divine Duality

The ***Law of Divine Duality*** is rooted in the Hermetic Law of Gender, which teaches that gender is a universal principle manifesting in all planes of existence, both seen and unseen. Far beyond physical definitions, this law represents a spiritual duality that exists within all creation, where both masculine and feminine energies are present and essential. The masculine embodies qualities of action, initiation, and purpose—the magnetic yet active force. In contrast, the feminine encompasses qualities of receptivity, intuition, and nurturance—the electric yet receptive force. Together, these forces are not oppositional but complementary, working in tandem to bring about creation, transformation, and evolution.

In revering the masculine and feminine, we recognize that both forces are required for balance, honoring their expression not only within ourselves but throughout the universe. The Law of Gender implies that all beings, regardless of physical gender, hold these energies within, allowing them to access the traits of each for spiritual growth. This duality is seen in archetypes throughout history—Osiris and Isis, Thoth and Ma'at—where masculine and feminine forces co-create in harmony.

Understanding the ***Law of Gender*** allows us to see how this interplay of forces gives rise to rhythm and flow, the natural cycles that sustain life. This principle operates on all planes of existence, including the mental plane, where the masculine and feminine energies are expressed within the mind. Here, the masculine corresponds to the objective, conscious mind—the active and initiating aspect. The feminine aligns with the subjective, subconscious mind—the receptive, intuitive, and passive aspect. Together, they form a dualistic mental structure, creating a balanced interplay essential for creativity and self-discovery.

This duality extends to the atomic level, where negative particles cluster around a positive core, symbolizing the feminine and masculine principles uniting to generate the atom. This metaphysical concept mirrors the dynamics of creation, showing us that when these energies interact, they generate new realities, ideas, and experiences. In practical terms, we observe this in business and creative endeavors, where masculine principles of action and direction blend with feminine energies of intuition and receptivity, giving rise to innovations, companies, and shared realities.

When we integrate these energies within ourselves, we amplify our vibrational frequency, aligning with the universal rhythm and cultivating a deeper spiritual understanding. By honoring both masculine and feminine aspects within us, we harmonize with the essence of creation itself, embodying the sacred balance that sustains existence on all levels.

Romans 1:20 offers a relevant perspective, stating, *"For since the creation of the world, God's invisible qualities—His eternal power and divine nature—have been clearly seen, being understood from what has been made, so that people are without excuse."* This verse suggests that the divine qualities, seen in the natural balance of the universe, reflect a harmonious duality present in all of creation. Just as the masculine and feminine energies work in tandem, this harmony signifies the divine order imbued within every aspect of life.

Metaphysically, the *Law of Divine Duality* resonates with the vibrational frequencies of divine energy, aligning us with the cosmic dance of masculine and feminine forces. This duality is expressed as the balance of magnetic and electric energies—the active and the receptive, the Creator and the Creation. Embracing both energies, we embody the principle of gender as outlined in ancient teachings, which reveal that all creation is born from the union of these complementary forces. Attuning ourselves to the expressions of these forces allows us to harmonize with the flow of creation, channeling their power and grace to elevate our own lives.

Philosophically, the *Law of Divine Duality* highlights the order, beauty, and balance intrinsic to the universe. Revering both the masculine and feminine encourages us to see beyond physical gender, recognizing their higher qualities—wisdom, courage, compassion, and love—as ideals toward which we strive. Ancient archetypes, like Osiris and Isis or Thoth and Ma'at, embody the harmony and cooperation between these forces. By honoring these qualities, we nurture virtues that guide us toward personal growth and enlightenment, reflecting a commitment to our own evolution as we seek to manifest the Creator's love and wisdom within ourselves.

To embrace the *Law of Divine Duality* is to honor the sacred balance that exists within and around us. Recognizing the value of both masculine and feminine aspects of divinity, we become conduits for their grace and strength, embodying their harmonious power. Through this reverence, we draw closer to our highest potential, establishing a harmonious relationship with the sacred balance of existence and aligning ourselves with the divine purpose embedded within creation.

Chapter 39: The Law of Humility

Humility is the recognition of our place within the vast expanse of the divine order, as taught by the ***Law of Humility***. This law invites us to approach life with an open mind, understanding that growth is an ongoing process and that every experience holds lessons. **James 4:10** speaks to this virtue: *"Humble yourselves before the Lord, and He will lift you up."* Humility, therefore, is not about diminishing our worth but about remaining grounded, aware of our evolving nature, and receptive to the guidance that lifts us to new heights.

Metaphysically, humility is an acknowledgment that we are vessels through which divine energy flows. We are not the originators of this energy but rather its caretakers and channels. By embodying humility, we open ourselves to the higher wisdom that reveals itself when we let go of ego and pride. This allows us to recognize that there is always more to learn, more ways to grow, and endless opportunities for mastery. Importantly, humility does not mean being passive or lacking ambition. Some may confuse humility with being docile or reserved, but in reality, humility coexists with fierce dedication and a relentless pursuit of excellence. It is about being aware that true strength and accomplishment are enhanced when we are open to continual growth and learning, embracing each new challenge with gratitude and resilience.

Philosophically, humility reflects a profound self-awareness and the understanding that, while we are capable of great achievements, we are also part of something far greater than ourselves. Ancient teachings suggest that humility is essential for developing virtue and wisdom. This perspective generates a sense of respect for the interconnectedness of all things, encouraging us to remain vigilant for insights and truths that deepen our understanding. Humility invites us to engage fully in our endeavors, blending assertiveness with receptivity, as we contribute to a collective, divine purpose. Even as we strive for excellence and pursue our goals with fervor, we are called to remain grounded, recognizing that humility doesn't mean sacrificing ambition but instead supports a balanced, meaningful pursuit of success.

To live by the ***Law of Humility*** is to walk the path of continuous learning, openness, and reverence for the sacredness of life. Humility allows us to be both strong in our accomplishments and receptive to the lessons that come with success and failure alike. We are called to pursue our goals with tenacity, recognizing that success is earned through diligent effort. True growth requires the balanced perspective of humility. By embodying this virtue, we cultivate a grounded sense of self, aligned with the divine purpose that guides our growth and development. Through humility, we remain anchored in grace, learning from each experience as we journey toward spiritual fulfillment.

Chapter 40: The Law of Integrity

The *Law of Integrity* serves as a powerful reminder that true success is rooted in honesty, transparency, and adherence to moral principles. Achieving with integrity challenges us to pursue our goals with steadfast commitment to ethical standards, even in a world where shortcuts and deception often masquerade as achievements. **Proverbs 10:9** resonates with this, stating, *"Whoever walks in integrity walks securely, but whoever takes crooked paths will be found out."* This reinforces the idea that achievements built on dishonesty are unsustainable, while those founded on integrity stand the test of time.

Metaphysically, the *Law of Integrity* aligns us with the high vibrational energies of divine truth and order. Integrity is the alignment of our actions with our inner values and spiritual purpose, ensuring that we attract only what is meant for our highest good. As we pursue our goals with honor, we naturally tap into the divine flow, gaining access to wisdom, guidance, and resources that are in harmony with the universal laws. Integrity provides us with a stable foundation, allowing us to move forward confidently, backed by the strength of divine alignment.

Philosophically, the *Law of Integrity* represents a commitment to authenticity and accountability. In ancient teachings, integrity was regarded as a central tenet of personal development, a trait that promotes a harmonious relationship between one's intentions, actions, and the outcomes they create. Integrity ensures that our accomplishments are meaningful and durable, free from the taint of deceit. By embodying integrity, we ensure that our success is both honorable and sustainable, creating a legacy that reflects the values we hold dear. This principle reflects the importance of achieving by using legitimate means, demonstrating that real success does not require manipulation or exploitation but rather a dedication to high standards and ethical actions.

To live by the *Law of Integrity* is to commit to a path where each step is taken with honesty, honor, and respect for others. Integrity magnifies our efforts, drawing us closer to the divine source of all wisdom and strength. When we achieve with integrity, we ensure that every accomplishment stands as a testament to our character, radiating the truth and goodness that define a life in alignment with Ma'at. In doing so, we serve not only ourselves but also contribute to a world where success is not measured solely by personal gain, but by the positive impact and enduring legacy we leave behind.

Chapter 41: The Law of Self-Reliance

The *Law of Self-Reliance* speaks to the power of independence, the importance of cultivating one's own strengths, and the pursuit of excellence. This law embodies the spirit of self-mastery and faith in oneself as a vessel of divine potential. **Ecclesiastes 9:10** resonates with this ideal, stating, *"Whatever your hand finds to do, do it with all your might, for in the realm of the dead, where you are going, there is neither working nor planning nor knowledge nor wisdom."* This verse emphasizes the dedication and diligence that lead to true success through one's own efforts.

Metaphysically, this principle reflects the understanding that our unique talents and abilities are sacred gifts, intended for growth and self-fulfillment. By honing in on these gifts, we align ourselves with the higher order of creation, demonstrating our commitment to fulfilling our divine purpose. Our abilities are expressions of the creator's energy, and through the diligent cultivation of these abilities, we contribute positively to our lives and to the broader world. By advancing through our own abilities, we engage in a sacred process of co-creation, where our individual strengths amplify the creative flow, manifesting success and spiritual progress.

Philosophically, the *Law of Self-Reliance* builds self-determination and accountability. Ancient wisdom teaches that true success is achieved by those who actively develop their skills and harness their inner resources. This perspective emphasizes that the journey to mastery requires both discipline and faith in our inherent potential. By progressing on our own terms, we build a strong foundation for success, free from dependency on external forces. This form of advancement allows us to become the architects of our own destiny, grounded in the understanding that we are powerful creators, aligned with a divine source.

To live by the *Law of Self-Reliance* is to embrace the role of a co-creator with the divine, recognizing that we have been endowed with the strength and intelligence to shape our path. When we rise to the challenges of life with an unwavering commitment to personal growth and excellence, we honor the sacred responsibility of living in alignment with our higher purpose. Through self-reliance, we affirm our connection to the divine, advancing not only for our own benefit but for the enrichment of the entire cosmic unity of which we are a part.

Chapter 42: The Law of Embracing The All

The **Law of Embracing The All** is the ultimate principle, the culmination of all other laws. This principle speaks to the profound truth of unity, where we recognize our interconnectedness with all of existence. It embodies the embrace of the Creator, the universe, and the divine essence within ourselves. As the *Kybalion* teaches, we **The All** is the infinite and unknowable source of all things, beyond time, space, and limitation. Although it is infinite and beyond full comprehension, this law invites us to consciously seek awareness of **The All** with every fiber of our being, reaching for understanding in every energy point of our existence. To embrace **The All** is to open ourselves to the entirety of creation and to understand that we are integral parts of a greater whole.

Colossians 1:17 states, *"He is before all things, and in Him all things hold together."* This speaks to the unifying essence of the divine, holding all of existence in a sacred balance. Additionally, **Acts 17:28** declares, *"For in him we live and move and have our being."* Together, these verses reflect the ultimate truth that we are both sustained by and connected to **The All**, embracing the totality of creation as an inseparable part of our own existence.

Metaphysically, the **Law of Embracing the All** invites us to become conscious of the principle that creation exists as an image within the mind of **The All**. Rooted in the understanding that "the universe is mental," this law suggests that everything we experience is part of a vast mental projection, held within the boundless consciousness of **The All**. As we attune ourselves to this principle, we begin to realize that the distinctions we perceive between ourselves and the universe are illusions. By polarizing our minds towards this awareness, we expand our perception of self, aligning our individual consciousness with the greater cosmic mind. Embracing **The All** is thus a journey of internal resonance, where we harmonize with the infinite mental projection of creation, merging our awareness with the oneness that sustains all existence.

In this way, the principle of embracing **The All** signifies the end of separation, bringing harmony between the inner and outer worlds. It is the realization that every thought, feeling, and action is an expression of the divine. By seeing ourselves in all others and all others within ourselves, we dissolve the boundaries of ego, and our awareness ascends to a higher state of universal understanding.

Philosophically, embracing **The All** is about acknowledging the inherent unity and divine order present in all things. Ancient wisdom teaches that life is a continual dance of dualities—light and darkness, creation and destruction, divine feminine and masculine energies—all harmonized within **The All**. Each of the *42 laws* we have explored serves as a pathway to understand this unity, illustrating the values and virtues that uphold the cosmic order. Applying these 42 laws positions us to face the weighing of the heart, where we align ourselves with Ma'at. By embodying these ideals, we approach a state where our hearts are balanced with truth, in preparation for the 42 confessions, signifying a life lived in harmony with divine order.

In embracing **The All**, we integrate the lessons of compassion, humility, truth, balance, and wisdom. This grand culmination emphasizes that our journey is not just about individual fulfillment but also about contributing to the greater harmony of the cosmos. As divine beings, we are tasked with embodying these principles, achieving mastery not for personal gain but for the upliftment of all creation. To live by this law is to participate actively in the co-creation of reality, allowing the divine presence to shine through us in every moment.

To align with *The All* is to accept our role as both individual expressions and integral components of the divine source. It is the recognition that all things—our thoughts, our actions, our very lives—are reflections of a grander, infinite purpose. By living in alignment with *The All*, we become vessels for divine energy, instruments of universal love, and catalysts for positive transformation. This commitment to *The All* is a pledge to live in accordance with the highest truths, knowing that we are, and have always been, one with the Creator and all of existence.

In honoring the *Law of Embracing The All*, we move beyond the illusions of separation, reflecting the unity, purpose, and divine essence that flow through every aspect of life. We are both creators and creations, actively shaping our destinies while honoring the oneness that binds all things. As we conclude the journey through these 42 laws, we understand that each law is but a facet of *The All*, guiding us toward a deeper, more profound relationship with the ultimate reality.

This final Law — The *Law of Embracing The All*—is both the beginning and the end, the realization of our divine sovereignty, and the promise of our ongoing spiritual journey. By aligning with *The All*, we become one with the universal flow, attuning ourselves to the eternal essence of life and fulfilling the sacred purpose that guides us toward love, truth, and unity with the divine. By following these 42 principles, we are guided, and through this guidance, we bring joy.

Conclusion: Walking the Path of Divine Wisdom

As we arrive at the culmination of this journey through *The 42 Laws of Wisdom* and their complementary biblical verses, we find ourselves standing at the doorway to a deeper understanding. This path we've traversed is more than just a collection of teachings; it's a living, evolving guide designed to inspire a life of integrity, purpose, and divine alignment. The principles of Ma'at, along with the insights from biblical scripture, offer a roadmap toward harmony, unity, and spiritual growth across all facets of life.

Each of these *laws* invites us to embody virtues that honor the divine, guiding us toward a balanced existence in harmony with ourselves, each other, and the greater cosmos. Whether through acts of ***truth, balance, or reverence,*** we are continually reminded of our path as one of reflection, growth, and alignment with higher truths. By embracing these principles alongside the expanded wisdom, we are drawn beyond the ordinary, awakening to the divine potential within and the greater unity that binds all existence.

Throughout this book, we have delved into the metaphysical, philosophical, and esoteric dimensions of each Law, constructing an intricate framework of wisdom that bridges ancient teachings with the timeless nature of spiritual truth. These laws are not merely for individual transformation; they are a call to co-create a harmonious world, grounded in compassion, understanding, and universal love. Together, these principles empower us to live in alignment with the sacred and serve as vessels of divine light.

As you continue your own journey, may these teachings be sources of light, guiding you toward a life filled with virtue, honor, and boundless love. Let them remind you of the divine essence within, calling you to embody your highest self and radiate that light to others. These laws aim to guide one towards a life of successful living, whether it be personal, interpersonal, educational, or entrepreneurial. Through these principles, may you walk with clarity and reverence, forever connected to *The All*.

www.ingramcontent.com/pod-product-compliance
Lightning Source LLC
Chambersburg PA
CBHW070809230426
43665CB00017B/2544